THE BATTLE OF THE V-WEAPONS
1944-45

THE BATTLE OF THE V-WEAPONS

V-WEAPONS

1944-45

BY

BASIL COLLIER

William Morrow & Company

New York, 1965

TO THE MEMORY OF

RODERIC HILL

CONTENTS

ILLUSTRATIONS

following page 128

MAPS

DIAGRAMS

I

Genesis

In the darkness before dawn on Tuesday, June 13, 1944, a small
aircraft flew from France to England, gaining height and speed
as it crossed the Channel. Passing over the stretch of coast
where Hitler's troops had failed to land in 1940, it continued
towards London, making 'a swishing sound' and emitting a
bright glow aft. By the time it reached the North Downs the
swishing sound had changed to a rattle graphically compared
by one observer with the noise made by a Model-T Ford going
up a hill. A few minutes later the aircraft dived into the ground
at Swanscombe, a village between Dartford and Gravesend and
about twenty miles east of Charing Cross.

There was a loud explosion, but no one was hurt. No sur-
vivors emerged to face interrogation, no bodies were extricated
from the wreckage. The machine was crewless.

When the British public learned in course of time that pilotless aircraft were being sent to vex them, this new twist to the
wizard war which stemmed from the German use of radio
beams in 1940 was generally regarded as a characteristic
example of Hitler's talent for disagreeable innovations. At the
same time there was something unnatural, something almost
supernatural, about the descent of the missiles on a great city,
which made the experience particularly unnerving even for
men and women who had stood worse ordeals in the
past.

Within ten weeks of the Swanscombe incident over a million

Londoners moved to the country at their own expense, in addition to more than a quarter of a million who travelled free of charge under government schemes for the voluntary withdrawal of school children and of younger children and their mothers. It was as if people recognised, fourteen months before Hiroshima and three months before the first long-range rocket fell near London, that they were seeing the dawn of a new age in which the old idea that part of a soldier's duty was to spare non-combatants would be finally thrown overboard.

If there was sound sense behind this verdict, the fact remains that the new development came as no surprise to the authorities. Long before the first pilotless aircraft was despatched across the Channel by a launching-crew far from confident that it would not turn and smite them, the British government were taking steps to checkmate German attempts to bring the missiles into use, and to lessen their effectiveness if they were used. So far were the air defences from being taken by surprise that, even in the dark, the Swanscombe missile was recognised and reported as a pilotless aircraft almost as soon as it crossed the coast.

Nor was bombardment of a hostile capital with such missiles by any means a novel conception when Hitler decided to put it into practice. Had the Führer wished to disclaim responsibility for thinking up a means of attack which added a new terror to existence, he might have pointed out that the idea of using jet-propelled pilotless aircraft to carry explosive charges into enemy territory occurred to the mind of man at least a quarter of a century before he came to power.

So far as is known, the first man to conceive and describe in detail a missile broadly similar to that used a generation later by the Germans was René Lorin, a French artillery officer who published a brief account of the matter immediately after the First World War.* Lorin claimed that his work on the subject

* René Lorin, *L'Air et la Vitesse* (Paris, 1919).

began in 1907, two years before Blériot made the first cross-Channel flight and four years before an Italian aviator gave mankind its first glimpse of an unattractive future by bombing the Turkish lines in the course of a Turco-Italian dispute in Tripoli. Before and during the 1914–18 war Lorin urged that long-range missiles should be developed for the purpose of bombarding such objectives as Berlin. He proposed as a suitable missile a pilotless aircraft stabilised by gyroscopes, propelled by some such means as a ram-jet or preferably a pulse-jet, and guided by radio from a master-aircraft which would stay out of reach of the defences. Many years later all these features, by that time scarcely novelties, turned up either in the German pilotless aircraft or in the Henschel 293 glider-bomb used by the Luftwaffe against Allied shipping in 1943.

Lorin had his own ideas of the lines on which a suitable pulse-jet might be constructed, but more sophisticated designs were available from other sources. On April 10, 1907, Victor de Karavodine, an inventor of whom little is known, was granted a patent for a pulse-jet which used a low-pressure supercharger to pump mixture into the combustion-chamber and a sparking-plug to ignite it.* A few years later Georges Marconnet, a Belgian who was no star-gazing visionary but a practical engineer with a sound commercial reputation, patented a whole series of jet-propulsion systems which he described as particularly suitable for aeroplanes and airships.† One of them was remarkably like the propulsion-unit afterwards used for the German pilotless aircraft. There is reason to believe that the German pulse-jet was, in fact, an independent invention, but that does not mean that its designers may not have been

---

* French Patent No. 374,124. The specification was lodged in Paris on April 9, 1906.

† French Patent No. 412,478. Marconnet stated when he lodged his specification in Paris on February 10, 1910, that he had applied on February 17, 1909, for a Belgian patent.

influenced, even without knowing it, by ideas which stemmed in the first place from Marconnet's work.

Between the wars, and especially in the nineteen-thirties, jet-propulsion and pilotless flight were studied in several countries, but inventors concerned with the one were not necessarily interested in the other. The British developed the pilotless De Havilland Queen Bee as a radio-controlled target aircraft. In Germany a pilotless machine intended for photographic reconnaissance reached the prototype stage by 1939 and flew successfully at Rechlin. Both machines, however, had orthodox piston-engines. Students of jet-propulsion were more interested, as a rule, in finding a successor to the piston-engine as a propellant for high-performance fighters than in applying their talents to winged missiles which seemed to have no immediate bearing on their problems.

Even so, other aspects of jet-propulsion were not entirely neglected. Between 1930 and the outbreak of the Second World War the German inventor Paul Schmidt designed and developed a pulse-jet, the Schmidt duct, which could be considered a logical step forward from the pioneering work of Lorin and Marconnet. A rival, the Argus duct, was a product of the design staff of the aero-engine firm of Argus Motorenwerke under the technical direction of Fritz Gosslau. Both were demonstrated in 1939, but little more was heard of them for the time being, presumably because of the difficulty of finding a practical use for propulsion systems which threatened to have only a short working life unless they could be further developed and improved. Schmidt suggested as early as the middle thirties that his invention should be used to propel a 'flying torpedo', but the response was disappointing. A later proposal was that pulse-jets should be installed in gliders so that pilots could use them intermittently to take evasive action. When Argus were invited, shortly before the outbreak of war, to submit proposals for a pilotless missile with a range of three hundred and fifty miles, they did not contemplate using the Argus duct, but suggested a piston-engine or alternatively a turbo-jet or a ducted fan.

Possibly the Argus project might have stayed in the files of the German Air Ministry for the rest of the war if the British Bomber Command had not chosen, in the early spring of 1942, to initiate a new programme of fire-raising by attacking Lübeck, the old Hanseatic city in Schleswig-Holstein. Incensed by the damage done to Lübeck's mediaeval buildings, Hitler ordered that 'terror attacks of a retaliatory nature' should be made on British cities other than London, and that these should supplement raids on ports and industry.* The 'Baedeker raids' which followed did a fair amount of damage, especially at Bath, York and Exeter, but they showed how markedly the hitting-power of German bomber units in the West had declined since 1941. The Luftwaffe was able to sustain a respectable effort against British cities only by moving units from the Mediterranean theatre at the height of its attacks on Malta, and the bombing of even supposedly foolproof targets was sometimes wildly inaccurate. While, for example, two attacks on Norwich were reasonably successful, on a third occasion less than two tons out of a hundred and thirteen tons of bombs aimed at the city fell within its boundaries, and none at all on built-up areas. Again, when seventy tons of high-explosive were aimed at Grimsby on the night of May 29, none hit the target and only twenty-eight tons were counted on land within a radius of fifty miles. Furthermore, the attackers suffered fairly heavy casualties, losing about forty aircraft in fourteen raids on Exeter, Bath, Norwich, York, Cowes, Hull, Poole, Grimsby and Canterbury between the last week in April and the end of May. This was hard going for a bomber force capable at best of an all-out effort of about two hundred sorties.

Not surprisingly, the spring of 1942 seemed to the Argus

* Führer Headquarters Signal No. 55 672/42 dated April 14, 1942.

firm a good time to ask the Air Ministry whether there was still life in the pilotless-aircraft project discussed in 1939. They were told that the project must not be allowed to drop, but that bottlenecks in the radio industry might rule out large-scale production of radio-controlled missiles.

Outwardly, this might not seem a very promising reply. In reality, circumstances had changed so much since the beginning of the war that it was more encouraging than it looked. With London less than a hundred miles from German-held territory, an expensive piston-engine or a still more expensive turbo-jet would no longer be needed for a missile whose useful life would be over in half an hour. Nor was it necessary that the missiles should be radio-controlled in order to hit so large a target at such close quarters. Another factor which promised a warm welcome from the Luftwaffe for a new means of hitting back at Britain was that the long-range rocket on which the German Army had been working since long before the war was at last beginning to shape well after many setbacks. Early in June a stage was reached at which trial launchings of the rocket in substantially its definitive form could begin. Should they be successful, an alternative weapon which enabled the Luftwaffe to keep its end up without making serious inroads on production of orthodox aircraft would be a boon to airmen determined not to let the soldiers steal their thunder if they could help it.

Thus the climate of official opinion that spring and summer tended to be more favourable to pilotless aircraft as offensive weapons than at any earlier stage of the war. Nor were Paul Schmidt and the Argus designers the only men on the creative side of the industry who believed by 1942 that such missiles had a future. Robert Lusser, an aeronautical engineer who had been in touch with Argus before taking up a post with Fieseler Flugzeugbau of Kassel, was keenly interested in the Argus project and carried his acquaintance with it to his new firm.

At the end of March Lusser wrote to Argus acknowledging that credit for suggesting the pilotless aircraft then under discussion belonged to them. But Argus were makers of aero-engines, while Fieseler were experienced designers and constructors of air-frames, whose Argus-powered Fieseler 196 (the *Storch* or Stork) was one of the most successful light aircraft ever made. Alive to the advantages of once more pooling their resources, the two firms agreed to develop the pilotless aircraft as a joint undertaking. A third firm, Askania, was brought in to work on the control mechanism, and an Air Ministry official, Staff-Engineer Brée, was appointed to co-ordinate the project on the ministry's behalf. Presumably so that Dr Schmidt's contribution to the study of jet-propulsion as applied to pilotless aircraft should not go unrecognised, the valve-mechanism of the Schmidt duct was combined with the remaining features of the Argus duct in the design ultimately accepted by Brée and his superiors.

On June 19, 1942, representatives of Argus and Fieseler attended a conference at the Air Ministry to discuss the future of the project. The chair was taken by Field-Marshal Erhard Milch, a veteran of the first-war flying corps who combined the posts of Inspector-General of the Luftwaffe, Director-General of Equipment, and Secretary of State for Air under Reichsmarschall Göring as Commander-in-Chief and Air Minister. Dr Gosslau, who represented Argus, outlined his conception of the weapon and backed his oral description with a sketch drawn on the spot on a sheet of Air Ministry paper. By the end of the meeting Milch ruled that the highest priority should be given to development and production of the missile.

Thus encouraged, the experts hoped that a delay of eighteen months would see their brain-child in action. In the outcome, almost exactly two years elapsed before a rather shaky start could be made to an offensive which scarcely came up to their expectations. Nevertheless they were hardly to blame if they were too sanguine. Few Germans could have been expected to foresee in 1942 the enormous difficulties that lay ahead.

At first called the Fieseler 103, the missile was later renamed the FZG. 76, a designation intended to baffle Allied agents and intelligence officers by suggesting that the function of the aircraft was to serve as a target or target-tower for anti-aircraft gunners. The ruse was not entirely successful, if only because few people, even in Germany, knew what the letters meant. (They stood, in fact, for *Flakzielgerät* or anti-aircraft artillery apparatus, but were widely thought to stand for *Fernzielgerät* or long-distance target apparatus.) *Vergeltungswaffe 1* or Reprisal Weapon No. 1 (whence V-1) was a name used only after the missile went into service. Other names applied to an object which seems to have struck many people as combining elements of the sinister and the comic included flying bomb, buzz bomb, doodle bug, and *Kirschkern* or cherry stone.

Early in December, 1942, Gerhard Fieseler of the firm of that name gave the embryo weapon its first practical trial by launching an unpowered prototype from a Focke-Wulf 200 aircraft at Peenemünde, the joint army-air force experimental station near Swinemünde at which the army were developing the long-range rocket. The first ground-launched missile was fired from a ramp, also at Peenemünde, on Christmas Eve and flew nearly a mile and three-quarters. An accuracy of half a mile on either side of the point of aim at a range of a hundred and fifty miles was achieved in later tests, but these figures threw a rather uncertain light on the ultimate performance of the weapon. Questions yet to be answered were to what extent mass-produced missiles assembled by indifferent or reluctant workers would stand comparison with prototypes or limited-production models, and whether the same attention to detail could be expected of units in the field as of picked crews under expert supervision.

At first inclined to regard the pilotless aircraft and the long-range rocket as alternative rather than complementary weapons, Hitler decreed while both were still under development that a special commission should sit in judgment on them and decide between the two. A crucial stage was reached when the commission visited Peenemünde to see things for themselves. The rival experts and their respective sponsors vied with each other to leave their guests with rosy recollections of the visit, optimism flourished, and in due course the commissioners recorded the opinion that both projects should be pursued.

By the summer of 1943 preparations to begin mass-production of the pilotless aircraft at the Volkswagen factory at Fallersleben were well advanced. As always when a new and complex product of the drawing-board and the research-bay was on the eve of taking what potential users hoped would be its definitive shape, the problem for the men at the top was to decide when to halt development, finalise the design, and make it clear to experts who pleaded for just one more modification that they would have to wait until a second edition was due to roll off the machines. At an unlucky moment for the Germans, the hazards of war brought the Fieseler works at Kassel to the top of the Allied list of aircraft factories scheduled for attack. The bombing of Kassel held up deliveries of limited-production models for a few days. This in turn delayed the testing of modifications due to be tried out on limited-production models before they were adopted or discarded. It also gave the experts another day or two to think up further modifications which their superiors were understandably reluctant to veto without trial. In the outcome production at Fallersleben did not start until late September, less than three months before active operations were due to begin according to the provisional programme sketched in 1942.

Nevertheless the armed forces went ahead with preparations on the assumption that both the FZG. 76 and the A-4 rocket would be ready in time to give the British a nice surprise at

Christmas. Flakregiment 155 (W), the unit formed for the purpose of aiming pilotless aircraft at Britain, began training in the summer at Zinnowitz, on the island of Usedom conveniently close to Peenemünde. Towards the end of October forward elements of the regiment moved to Northern France. By that time locations for ninety-six launching-sites had been chosen, and work on the sites was so far advanced that all but a few were expected to be ready by the middle of December. Features common to all the sites included a ramp from which the missiles would be catapulted by an auxiliary launching-device which gave a powerful initial thrust, and a square building which long puzzled British intelligence officers. In addition each site was provided with a number of tunnel-like buildings in which the missiles and their wings could be stored before final assembly. To give some protection against blast in case of air attack, these buildings were slightly curved at one end.

To complete the programme, massive concrete structures at Siracourt (near Saint-Pol) and Lottinghem (near Saint-Omer) were built to serve as bomb-proof launching points usable even in the worst conditions. A third structure at Equeurdreville, one of several intended in the first place for long-range rockets, was afterwards added to these two.

The higher command of the organisation concerned with long-range bombardment took shape in the autumn and early winter. In September Major-General Walter Dornberger, the German Army's leading authority on long-range ballistic weapons and father of the A-4 rocket, was given two distinct posts which made him responsible not only for co-ordinating development programmes with operational requirements but also for directing active operations. Having spent a great part of his career in charge of long-range rocket research and development at Peenemünde and formerly at Kummersdorf, Dornberger was not protected by his unrivalled knowledge and all-round ability from the charge that he lacked experience in the field. In December a seasoned artillery commander, Lieutenant-General Erich Heinemann, assumed overriding responsibility for active operations with both pilotless aircraft and long-range rockets, and in due course Dornberger, while still responsible for technical development and training, was replaced as commander of the rocket-firing troops by a new-comer to long-range ballistic missiles, Major-General Richard Metz. Throughout these changes Flakregiment 155 (W), the unit responsible for handling pilotless aircraft in the field, remained under its first and only commander, Colonel Wachtel, who became answerable in December to General Heinemann but had never been answerable to Dornberger and was not answerable to Metz.

General Heinemann did not take long to discover that he had been saddled with a thankless task. Metz reported that the A-4 rocket was nothing like ready to be entrusted to units in the field, and was openly critical of Dornberger and his training-programme. Even when allowances were made for his lack of sympathy with his predecessor and unconcealed eagerness to exchange his unsought post for one more congenial, there was no escaping the conclusion that any idea of opening a long-range offensive against Britain by the end of the year, or even by the following midsummer, must be abandoned.

As for the pilotless aircraft, Heinemann reckoned that it might be ready by the late spring or early summer of 1944. If this estimate seemed encouraging in comparison with his verdict on the rocket, the same could hardly be said of the rest of his conclusions. One of his first moves after he took up his appointment was to make a tour of the launching-sites in Northern France. He found that, to hasten the work, extensive use had been made of local labour. At some sites, French contractors as well as French workmen had been employed. Through no fault of Wachtel's, little regard had been paid to security, and the purpose as well as the location of the sites were matters of common gossip and conjecture. Furthermore, the installations seemed to Heinemann needlessly elaborate. Their distinctively-shaped buildings made them easily visible from the air, and they were highly vulnerable to bombing. The so-called protected sites at Siracourt and elsewhere could never nourish more than a small scale of attack, and in any case Heinemann had little faith in them.

Heinemann was too experienced a commander to risk a profitless dispute with his superiors by openly condemning the mania for the grandiose which had led to the expenditure of so much concrete at Siracourt and Lottinghem. Where the un-protected sites were concerned he felt no such compunction. Within a few weeks of his arrival he recommended that the whole programme should be radically overhauled, that work on the existing sites should be continued only as a blind, and that a fresh start should be made with an entirely new set of sites of a simpler and less distinctive pattern. His arguments were irresistible in face of the bombing offensive which the Allies opened early in December. Thus the months which ought, according to plan, to have seen the beginning of a powerful two-pronged assault on the United Kingdom found the authorities responsible for the rocket striving desperately to make their weapon fit for use, while those concerned with the pilotless aircraft chose new locations for their launching-ramps in the hope that supplies of missiles and equipment would be forthcoming soon enough for them to make a belated start in the following May or June.

2

Enigma

FROM the start, and even before the start, the trail of the German pilotless aircraft was overlaid, so far as British investigators were concerned, by that of the long-range rocket. The story of the search for the flying bomb becomes comprehensible only when it is understood that the discovery by British intelligence officers that the Germans were about to bombard the United Kingdom with winged missiles was largely a by-product of the search for the wingless missile which Hitler was also planning to bring into use, and which ultimately he did bring into use.

For practical purposes German interest in long-range precision rockets as weapons of bombardment began about ten years after the First World War, when officers of the Ordnance Branch of the German Army conceived the notion that such weapons might be used to offset a lack of artillery resulting from the Treaty of Versailles, and as a suitable means of delivering poison-gas if it should again be used in war. As early as 1923 Herman Oberth, a Transylvanian Saxon who still looked to the Fatherland, had suggested in a technical treatise that rockets using liquid fuels might attain the immensely long ranges needed for inter-planetary flight. His work came to the attention of highly-placed officers when he expanded his paper into a full-length book which appeared in 1929.

The future General Dornberger, who then held the rank of Captain and had spent three years acquiring a scientific background at the Technical High School in Berlin, joined the Ballistics and Munitions Section of the Ordnance Branch in 1931, and soon made his mark as an exponent of 'liquid' rockets. In 1934 he succeeded in launching two liquid-propelled rockets with gyroscopic stabilisers from the island of Borkum, off the North Sea coast. Encouraged by General von Fritsch, Commander-in-Chief of the German Army until his dismissal by Hitler in 1938, Dornberger and his staff produced in 1936 the long-term plan which laid the foundations for the A-4 rocket. Notwithstanding successful tests of the A-4 in 1942, which followed a long series of experiments with smaller rockets, the missile was, however, still far from ready for use when large-scale production of the cheaper and simpler flying bomb began in the autumn of 1943.

German technicians were known before the war to be interested in the application of rocketry to inter-planetary flight and other quasi-scientific uses, but the British government would seem to have received their first authentic warning that the military authorities were developing long-range rockets for warlike purposes when the famous Oslo Report reached them late in 1939. Soon after the outbreak of war the British Naval Attaché in Oslo was offered by an anonymous correspondent a report on German technical developments, the only stipulation being that the government should first affirm their willingness to receive it by causing a minute change to be made in the preamble to the B.B.C.'s German news broadcast on a particular evening. Appropriate orders were given to the announcer concerned, and early in November, 1939, the report arrived. It said, amongst much else, that the Germans were developing large rockets and that they had an important experimental station at Peenemünde.

From the start it was obvious that the writer of the Oslo Report was no ordinary secret agent or half-witted crank. The author of a paper which dealt with such a wide range of developments must either be an exceptionally well informed and highly qualified well-wisher to the Allied cause, or have been specially briefed by the German authorities to convey misleading information. In other words, the report was either a document of great value, or it was a hoax intended to divert attention from some project or projects of outstanding significance to less important or non-existent undertakings. If the Germans were developing, for example, an atom bomb, then their readiness to take the trouble to stage an elaborate deception would be understandable. And Germany must certainly be reckoned capable of making an atom bomb if her resources were fully developed and if it could be done at all. Her Czechoslovakian adventure had given her access to the uranium deposits at Joachimsthal, at that time the best-known in the world. She possessed, in Otto Hahn, a chemist who combined unrivalled understanding of the theoretical basis of nuclear fission with first-hand experience of the process in laboratory conditions.

Fortunately for humanity, Hahn was a convinced anti-Nazi who would rather have died than put a weapon of unprecedented power in Hitler's hands. Hoping and believing that accomplishment of the controlled chain-reaction needed for practical exploitation of the fission process would continue to elude his fellow-scientists for years to come if not for ever, he declared that success would be 'contrary to God's will'. Less fortunately, a number of refugee scientists in the United States believed in the summer of 1939 that Hitler would not have dared to defy the democracies as he had done since Munich unless he had a trump card up his sleeve. Concluding from a newspaper interview in which one of Hahn's associates had tried to warn the public of the dangers of a chain-reaction that Hahn had been made to impart his secrets to the Nazi authorities and that Hitler was on the eve of a new break-through, they decided to forestall him by putting their own knowledge at the disposal of the United States government, then still resolutely neutral. It was not, however, until 1942 that the British and United States governments agreed to pool their nuclear resources, thus putting the Allied military machine on the road to Hiroshima by way of Canadian uranium deposits.

Meanwhile events showed that some, at any rate, of the projects mentioned in the Oslo Report were anything but mythical. As the months went by, development after development made its due appearance. Dr R. V. Jones, a physicist who held a key position in the Intelligence organisation at the Air Ministry, said afterwards that 'in the few dull moments of the war' he used to turn to the Oslo Report to see what ought to be coming along next.

Nevertheless, for some years little attention was paid to the warning about long-range rockets, or to Peenemünde. The Baltic coast from Schleswig-Holstein to the Oder was first covered by photographic reconnaissance on October 29, 1940, when Flying-Officer S. J. Millen made a five-hour sortie in a new super-long-range Spitfire, chiefly for the purpose of discovering whether the Germans were assembling invasion craft in Baltic ports; but Millen appears to have received no special instructions about Peenemünde. The lukewarm interest shown in an establishment singled out for mention in the Oslo Report appears almost unbelievably startling until one reflects that not even Rechlin, the Luftwaffe experimental station where prototypes of new German aircraft were taken for their acceptance tests, was photographed until the war was well into its third year.

In the outcome the first significant cover of Peenemünde was obtained almost by chance. On May 15, 1942, Flight Lieutenant D. W. Steventon photographed Kiel and then flew on to Swinemünde. Approaching Swinemünde he noticed the aerodrome at Peenemünde, and decided that it was worth photographing. His photographs showed a number of large circular earthworks which at first attracted only passing interest from photographic interpreters, since no one had been specially briefed to study such constructions.

By the following spring the picture had changed considerably. In December, 1942, an agent whose reliability had yet to be assessed sent in the first of a series of reports which indicated, correctly, that trials of a long-range rocket had been held recently near Swinemünde. Early in 1943 reports from other sources linked these trials specifically with Peenemünde. The photographs taken in the previous May were then scrutinised with a new interest, and further cover was arranged. By April the interpreters, with four sets of photographs to work on, were able to point not only to the circular earthworks already noticed, but also to a large elliptical earthwork which looked something like a football stadium. In addition, there was evidence that prisoners of war acquainted with high-level service gossip current at the time of their capture were aware that the German High Command had at least one novel weapon in prospect.

At that point the British began to pay heavily for their lack of an inter-service organisation capable of collating intelligence from all sources with an authority recognised on all sides.

The Air Ministry had received all the information about German long-range rockets which had reached the country since the beginning of the war. Content to leave the detailed study of it to men whose job it was, and particularly to Dr Jones, who had proved his worth by unmasking the German target-finding radio beams in 1940, the few senior officers to whom Jones conveyed a word of warning accepted his assurance that he was on the track of the Peenemünde rocket and would tell them more when he knew more.

The War Office possessed exactly the same information, but the staff there viewed their responsibilities in a different light.

In April, 1943, they took steps which they could not be blamed for taking, but whose effect was none the less to draw a gigantic red herring across a trail already confused by the failure of some agents to distinguish between the long-range rocket and the flying bomb. In the first place the army officers immediately concerned, regarding a German rocket offensive as a more imminent danger than Jones thought it, put the salient facts and inferences before the Vice-Chief of the Imperial General Staff, Lieutenant-General A. E. Nye. General Nye in turn consulted Professor C. D. Ellis and Dr A. D. Crow, respectively Scientific Adviser to the Army Council and Director and Controller of Projectile Development in the Ministry of Supply, before circulating to the Vice-Chiefs and Chiefs of Staff a memorandum to which was annexed a speculative account of the kind of weapon the Germans might conceivably have in view. If Nye or his staff felt that they had to draw such a picture, it was natural that, before doing so, they should turn for guidance to advisers whom they would have consulted had a British long-range weapon project been in view. It happened, however, that British students of ballistics had had few opportunities in recent years of becoming familiar with special applications of liquid propulsion which were being studied behind the scenes in Germany, and to some extent in the United States. Nor was it normally part of the responsibilities of the Scientific Adviser to the Army Council or the Director of Projectile Development to fill gaps in the picture of German activities presented by the intelligence services, or to make such a detailed, day-to-day scrutiny of technical developments in foreign countries as intelligence officers might be expected to make. The outcome of the action taken in the War Office was not only that the alarm was sounded in high places before the nature of the threat had been established, but also that statesmen with no time to study the evidence at first hand received a misleading impression of what was in the wind.

Thereafter not merely two but three missiles competed for the attention of investigators. These were the A-4 rocket, the FZG. 76 pilotless aircraft or flying bomb, and the mythical rocket envisaged by British experts. Not surprisingly, since the search for a needle in a haystack can be expected to be even more protracted than usual if the needle is not there, attempts to drag the third into the light of day absorbed a disproportionate share of the effort which might more profitably have been devoted to the discovery of the first and second. Moreover, notions of the rocket even more far-fetched than those outlined in Nye's paper were soon current in Whitehall. Assuming, because they had been told so, that cordite was the most probable propellant, and assuming also that an immense weight of cordite would be needed to give the stipulated range and that only a huge war-head could justify the expenditure of so much fuel and effort, intelligence officers devoted hundreds of man-hours to the quest for massive launching sites suitable for 60-ton rockets which would have to be brought by rail. At the same time, civil defence experts brooded on the problem of protecting Londoners against a hail of 10-ton war-heads, each capable of killing six hundred people at a stroke. Yet in fact the A-4 rocket weighed less than 13 tons with all its fuel aboard, was transportable by road, and could be fired with the aid of a movable stand from any firm and reasonably level surface as long as hard standings were available for the attendant vehicles.*

* After the war had ended General Dornberger himself seems to have gone so far as to claim that the rocket could have been launched from 'a bit of planking on a forest track, or the overgrown track itself'. In point of fact, where the Germans did use such locations when firing at Continental targets in 1944 and 1945, they thought it worth their while to provide concrete platforms for the launching-stand and concrete or corduroy hard standings for their vehicles. All but a very few of the rockets aimed at London between September, 1944, and March, 1945, were launched from prepared sites in, or on the outskirts of, the built-up area of The Hague. The sites in France from which the Germans hoped at one time to launch rockets at England in the summer of 1944 also had concrete platforms and hard standings. The rocket generated an initial thrust of twenty-five tons

As the sequel to misgivings aroused by the Nye memorandum, the War Cabinet secretariat suggested about the middle of April, 1943, that responsibility for investigating the problem posed by the long-range rocket should rest not with the intelligence staffs at either the War Office or the Air Ministry, but with one man who could devote a good deal of time to the work. The choice fell on Mr Duncan Sandys, Joint Parliamentary Secretary to the Ministry of Supply, son-in-law of the Prime Minister, and a willing skirmisher who had shown by his criticism of the authorities after the emergency deployment of the air defences in 1938 that he was not afraid to stick his neck out.

The appointment of a new investigator seemed a retrograde step to airmen who would have preferred that Dr Jones should be left to discover the secrets of the rocket in his own way. But the picture had another side. It was true that Mr Sandys was, to say the least, no better qualified than Dr Jones to deal with the intelligence problem, and indeed might seem more likely than Jones to be misled by the preconceptions of British experts, since his business hitherto had been with British rather than German weapons. On the other hand, as a member of the government he was in a good position to insist on countermeasures. Believing that his real job was not so much to find out exactly what the rocket was like as to satisfy himself that everything possible was done to counter it, he performed a valuable function by helping to ensure that the men at the top were not led astray by scoffers who suspected a mare's nest. Among the sceptics with whom he had to deal was the Prime Minister's Scientific Adviser Lord Cherwell, more widely known by his old name of Professor Lindemann. Rightly disbelieving in the existence of 60-ton rockets which the Germans

---

and the movable stand had to be firmly placed, so an unprepared forest track would scarcely have been suitable unless its surface happened to be exceptionally hard, smooth and level.

would find hard to use in face of Allied air superiority, Cherwell carried scepticism so far as to argue that they had no long-range rocket at all, and were pulling wool over the eyes of Sandys and his investigators in the hope of blinding them to other projects.

It remains true that neither Duncan Sandys nor anyone else had any clear idea in early May of what the Germans were doing, and that a tentative account of the rocket which he included in his first report in the middle of that month did help to foster exaggerated notions of the weight of the missile and its war-head. Whether the account did more harm than good by raising false clues and unnecessary fears, or more good than harm by emphasising the seriousness of the threat, can only be a matter of opinion.

Nor was it yet clear that the Germans were developing two distinct weapons. More perspicacious or a better guesser than most of his critics, Sandys asked when on May 9 he visited the Central Interpretation Unit at Medmenham, where air photographs were scrutinised, whether the Aircraft Section could point to any unidentified aircraft at Peenemünde which might square with the description of a 'remotely-controlled pilotless aircraft'. But Constance Babington Smith, the W.A.A.F. officer in charge of the section, could tell him nothing helpful since none of the existing cover was sharp enough or of large enough scale to give the kind of information that was needed.

If the false picture of the rocket which emerged from the Nye memorandum and the first of the Sandys reports led to a good deal of wasted effort, the jolt given to the Air Ministry by the appointment of an independent investigator over the head of Dr Jones did have the useful effect of making his superiors more receptive to the notion that one way of speeding the investigation might be to put more people to work on it and provide them with more material. Immediately after the appointment of Mr Sandys the Central Interpretation Unit received instructions to give 'the highest priority' to a special 'secret weapons' investigation. Wing Commander Hamshaw Thomas, one of their best men and a pioneer of photographic interpretation who had furnished General Allenby with reconnaissance material for his capture of Jerusalem in the First World War, was put in charge of it. Four interpreters, headed by Flight Lieutenant André Kenny, were assigned to the search for evidence of experimental work and production at Peenemünde and elsewhere. Peenemünde itself, which had been covered only some six to eight times between the outbreak of war and the beginning of June, 1943, was photographed no less than four times in that month alone, and arrangements were made for British and American reconnaissance aircraft to complete a programme which would give recent cover of the whole of the French coast from Cherbourg to the Belgian frontier.

Photographs brought back from Peenemünde on June 2 showed a tall object standing on a fan-shaped expanse of foreshore afterwards found to have been overlaid with asphalt. This was cautiously described as 'a thick vertical column about 40 feet high', but was in fact a rocket resting on its fins. Later cover, on June 23, revealed unmistakable rockets lying horizontally on road-vehicles within the confines of the stadium-like elliptical earthwork. But in some ways an even more important event which occurred that month was the arrival of a report from a source who described 'the secret weapon to be used against London' as 'an air-mine with wings, long-distance steering and a rocket-drive', and added that it was to be launched by catapult. That did not sound much like a supersonic long-range rocket, but it did sound rather like a flying bomb.

The Defence Committee (Operations) had, therefore, a good deal to discuss when, with Winston Churchill in the chair, they met on June 29 to consider the latest report from Mr Sandys. Lord Cherwell, as sceptical as ever, argued that the objects photographed on June 23 were dummies and that the whole story bore the marks of an elaborate cover-plan designed to conceal some genuine development such as a flying bomb. Sandys and Jones retorted that Peenemünde was an experimental station of great value to the Germans, and that they were hardly likely to stage a hoax whose probable effect, if it succeeded, would be to call down an attack upon the place. A small piece of evidence which helped to clinch the argument for Jones was a German Air Ministry circular about petrol coupons, in which Peenemünde was listed above experimental stations whose importance was beyond dispute.

After fairly lengthy debate the committee approved of a number of counter-measures proposed by Sandys, among them an attack on Peenemünde as soon as the nights were long enough. They dealt with the suggestion that preoccupation with the rocket might lead to the neglect of other dangers by inviting Mr Sandys to study, in association with Dr Jones, the application of jet-propulsion to aircraft, piloted or pilotless.

On the night of August 17 just under six hundred aircraft of Bomber Command set out to make the round trip of a thousand miles to Peenemünde and back. Forty failed to return, but substantial damage was done to buildings, and German casualties were heavy. Partly as a result of the raid, the Germans abandoned a plan to assemble rockets at Peenemünde, Friedrichshafen and Wiener Neustadt, and transferred all assembly to an underground factory at Niedersachswerfen, near Nordhausen in the Harz Mountains. On Hitler's orders, most trial launchings of the rocket were made thereafter at Blizna, in Poland. The move put the launching-teams out of harm's way so far as bombing was concerned, but helped British intelligence officers to keep a watch on their activities through the Polish underground. The rocket programme suffered another setback when a factory which made some of the special vehicles used for transporting, fuelling and servicing the missile was fortuitously destroyed in a raid on Hamburg, and was further delayed by technical troubles of which the hardest to cure was a structural weakness leading to a high proportion of premature bursts. Development of the flying bomb does not seem to have been much affected by the raid on Peenemünde, but it did suffer from the bottleneck caused by damage done at Kassel.

Meanwhile a growing body of evidence from secret sources testified to the existence of at least two German missiles. A highly circumstantial report received about the middle of August gave the A-4 rocket its correct designation and referred to a flying missile as a weapon distinct from it. At the end of the month a new source fell into the common error of confusing the flying bomb with the rocket, but went far to redeem his mistake by identifying the launching-regiment as Flakregiment 155 (W) and its commander as Colonel Wachtel. He added that the regiment would be deployed in France about the beginning of November and would man 108 catapults. Soon afterwards news of a missile which had landed on the Danish island of Bornholm, about eighty miles north-east of Peenemünde and roughly the same distance from Flakregiment 155 (W)'s training-area at Zinnowitz, helped to make it clear that the Germans were experimenting with pilotless aircraft of a kind which might well be suitable for launching from a catapult. Almost simultaneously the introduction of the Henschel 293 glider-bomb strengthened the case for the long-range rocket, since the author of the Oslo Report was proved right in predicting a glider-bomb and might therefore be right about the rocket.

Even so, the picture was still far from complete, and many of its features remained as incomprehensible as ever. Huge concrete structures revealed by photographic reconnaissance at Watten, Wizernes, Sottevast, Equeurdreville, Mimoyecques, Siracourt and Lottinghem were said by Allied agents to have something to do with secret weapons; but whether all were meant to serve the same purpose in spite of obvious differences between them, and whether they were connected with the rocket or the flying bomb, or with both, were baffling questions. Because the structures were very big, and because the rocket was believed also to be very big, it was tempting to assume that the two must be connected; but case-hardened intelligence officers rightly refused to make that assumption without further evidence.

A certain amount of further evidence was, in fact, forthcoming, and a good deal more was discovered about the 'large sites' in the course of the next few months. It was not, however, until after the capture of the sites by Allied troops in the summer of 1944 that all or most of their secrets were revealed. Their intended purposes, none of which they ever served, then turned out to be almost as diverse as their appearance. Watten, it was found, had been designed to provide facilities not only for the fuelling, servicing and launching of rockets with the minimum of interference from Allied aircraft, but also for the storage of the missiles and their fuel and the manufacture of liquid oxygen, at least seven tons of which were consumed for every rocket launched. Sottevast and Equeurdreville were broadly similar, but the second had been converted to a protected launching-site for flying bombs, while Siracourt and Lottinghem were always intended for that purpose. Wizernes, originally an underground store for rockets, took the place of Watten as an intended launching-site when Watten was so badly damaged by bombing as to be judged useless for all purposes except the production of liquid oxygen. As for Mimoyecques, the workings there were found, as had long been suspected, to have no connection with either the rocket or the flying bomb, and to have been built to house a multi-barrel long-range gun designed to pump out projectiles with collapsible fins and a calibre of six inches at a muzzle-velocity of roughly five thousand feet a second.

By early September Sandys had so much on his plate that he was glad to relinquish responsibility for studying jet-propulsion and pilotless aircraft to the Air Ministry. In the meantime a heavy attack on Watten by Fortresses of the United States Eighth Air Force on August 27, followed by a lighter attack on September 7, wrought such havoc that the eminent engineer Sir Malcolm McAlpine remarked, when photographs of the damaged site were shown to him, that the Germans would find it easier to start over again than attempt repairs.

Retaining his interest in the rocket, Sandys asked on October 21 for fresh reconnaissance of the whole of the part of Northern France from which long-range rockets seemed likely to be launched. The outcome was a spate of new photographs which the interpreters at Medmenham scrutinised with unquenchable zeal, but with no very clear idea of what they were to look for. With the possible exception of the 'large sites', whose role was doubtful, nothing had been found in Northern France which looked like evidence of preparations to launch large rockets. Nor did anyone yet know how much the rocket or its war-head weighed, or how it was propelled. Its dimensions could be assumed, with reservations, from those of the objects photo-graphed at Peenemünde, but these might not be complete, and British experts could only guess what was inside them or was meant to go inside them. Whether the definitive weapon was a single-stage or multi-stage missile, whether it rose under its own power or was launched from a projector, and whether the fuel was liquid or solid, were all questions still unanswered. Returning from a visit to the United States in the late summer, Mr I. Lubbock of the Asiatic Petroleum Company brought news of experiments with liquid fuels, and above all of the use of a pump to force them into the combustion-chamber of a rocket, which threw new light on the possibilities of liquid propulsion without recourse to the heavy compressed-air containers hitherto predicated. But there was no proof that the

Germans were in fact using such methods, and such evidence as could be gleaned from agents' reports and elsewhere was fragmentary and inconclusive. On the other hand, there *were* indications which seemed to justify a suspicion that the Germans might already have made about five hundred rockets.

At that stage new evidence arrived which seemed at first to make the picture even more confusing. Towards the end of October an agent in France reported that the firm of contractors which employed him was working on eight sites near Abbeville whose purpose he did not understand, but which he suspected of a connection with secret weapons. He added a valuable description of their whereabouts, and on November 3 all eight were photographed. The photographs showed that all the sites were very similar in layout and situation, but that they had reached different stages of completion. The most nearly finished of them was partly in a wood called the Bois Carré, near Yvrench, and each of the others was also partly in a wood. Unlike the 'large sites', none was served by rail-spurs or was even near a railway. Study of the photographs taken on November 3 and of earlier and later photographs of the same and other sites led to the conclusion that each site, when completed, would consist of a number of characteristic buildings more or less obscured from observers on the ground by trees, but plainly visible from the air. These included a rectangular concrete slab with a small concrete hut or shelter at one end and a row of concrete studs along each side of the other; a square building, also of concrete, with a twenty-two-foot opening across practically the whole width of one side; and a small number of curiously-shaped constructions gently curved in plan at one end, ten feet in width, and up to about two hundred and sixty feet in length. The standard number of these curved buildings, again made of concrete, seemed to be three, of which one was shorter than the other two. At all the sites near Abbeville, the longer axis of the rectangular slab was aligned on

London, and the square building was exactly in line with it and had its open side also facing towards London.

Seeing a resemblance between the long, narrow, windowless buildings and huge skis laid on their sides, Wing Commander Douglas Kendall of the Central Interpretation Unit called the new sites ski sites, and thereafter they were known by that name, or alternatively as Bois Carré sites after the type-station. But to give the sites a name was one thing; to know what they were for was another. One safe inference was that they were not for launching rockets so heavy that they had to come by rail. But were they for lighter rockets, or for flying bombs? And if they were for flying bombs, where were the rocket-sites which Kendall's opposite numbers in Whitehall were so insistent that he should find for them?

3

Climax and Anti-Climax

DURING the first week in November, 1943, the Sandys enquiry reached a peculiarly baffling stage. With the exception of Lord Cherwell and a few other diehards, most of the experts on whom Mr Sandys relied for technical guidance believed more or less firmly in the existence of the long-range rocket. Yet none of them could give a confident description of the missile, or assess its performance except in terms which those of them who did risk a forecast contrived, by an almost unique combination, to make at one and the same time exceedingly broad and exceedingly misleading. Nor could the ski sites be easily fitted into the picture of the rocket. The government thus faced the paradox that, while the tempo of counter-measures had quickened with the attacks on Peenemünde and Watten and demands for fresh reconnaissance, the nature of the threat which was being countered was in some ways more obscure than at the outset of the search.

In these circumstances, the Prime Minister asked the Minister of Aircraft Production, Sir Stafford Cripps, to try to find out whether the supposed secret weapons could reasonably be assumed to exist and, if he decided that they did exist, to do his best to define the threat that they presented.

At the first meeting summoned by Cripps, on November 8, Flight Lieutenant Kenny spoke of Peenemünde, the objects photographed there and the effects of the attack in August, and went on to deal with the 'large sites'. His descriptions showed that the sites were not all alike, and hence could not be assumed without further evidence to serve a common purpose.

Wing Commander Kendall then caused something of a stir by announcing that no less than nineteen ski sites had been located on reconnaissance photographs up to midnight on the previous day, and that in all probability more had been found by the time he was speaking. Thereupon Cripps adjourned the meeting for two days so as to give the interpreters time to complete their search and put their conclusions into shape.

By the time of the second meeting, twenty-six ski sites had been discovered, but their purpose was still uncertain. Nor were the scientists present able to throw much light on the long-range rocket. Some thought that it would turn out to be a two-stage missile entirely dependent on its own power, while others envisaged a single-stage projectile fired from some kind of mortar. On the whole the second school of thought prevailed, although there was no satisfactory evidence that the Germans were using mortars and a good deal of difficulty in reconciling the idea of insertion in a mortar with the fins seen on the rockets photographed at Peenemünde.

Nor was there convincing evidence to support the concept of a sixty-ton rocket, in which some of the scientists continued to believe. At the end of the enquiry Cripps reported that there was 'nothing impossible in designing a rocket of 60-70 tons to operate with a 10-ton war-head at a range of 130 miles', but he was not so rash as to assert that the Germans had in fact provided themselves with such a weapon. He also expressed the opinion that pilotless aircraft were a more immediate danger than long-range rockets.

Accordingly, the Central Interpretation Unit stepped up its search for aircraft which looked as if they might be pilotless. On November 13 Section Officer Babington Smith succeeded in finding, on exceptionally clear photographs of Peenemünde taken on June 23, a midget aircraft with a wing-span of twenty feet or so which she called provisionally the Peenemünde 20. Her discovery strengthened a growing conviction in Douglas Kendall's mind that the ski sites were meant for launching flying bombs and that the square building was designed to harbour a winged missile of just such dimensions.

On the ground that the problem of the rocket had entered a new phase, that the 'special enquiry' stage had passed and that there was a growing demand for counter-measures which could not conveniently be co-ordinated by a civilian, the Chiefs of Staff proposed a few days later, after consulting Mr Sandys, that the functions he had performed since April should be transferred to the Air Ministry. On· November 18 the Deputy Chief of the Air Staff, Air Marshal Norman Bottomley, succeeded Sandys as investigator-in-chief. Thus the search for the rocket came once more under the same aegis as the search for the flying bomb.

By the last week in November ninety-five ski sites had been identified. This came close to the hundred and eight catapults mentioned by the agent who named Colonel Wachtel as commander of the launching-regiment, and still closer to the ninety-six ski sites in fact planned by the Germans.

Meanwhile there was good reason to believe that a certain German signals unit concerned with radio beams and radar, which was known to be deployed on the Pomeranian coast and the islands of Rügen and Bornholm, was tracking pilotless aircraft launched from Zinnowitz and Peenemünde. Still awaiting a firm link between these activities and the ski sites, intelligence officers interested in the signals unit asked for photographic reconnaissance of Zinnowitz and especially of the radar installation which they suspected would be found there.

Good weather for air photography over Northern Germany was not very common in the early winter. On November 28, however, Squadron Leader John Merifield and his navigator,

Flying Officer Whalley, set off in a Mosquito from their base at Leuchars for Berlin, with the Baltic coast as an alternative objective. Finding the skies near Berlin as thick with cloud as other crews had found them in recent weeks, they turned north to photograph a miscellany of ports, aerodromes and other installations, winding up with Peenemünde.

At Medmenham three days later, Section Officer Babington Smith was drawing near the end of a long search through past cover of Peenemünde for more examples of the midget aircraft to which she had drawn attention a fortnight earlier. Her chief, Wing Commander Kendall, was in London, defending his theory that the ski sites were for flying bombs in face of scepticism from critics distressed by his failure to discover signs of preparations to launch sixty-ton rockets. Looking at photographs of an area which did not strictly concern her since it lay outside the limits of the aerodrome, she saw at the end of a road leading northwards to the Baltic shore a ramp banked up with earth, supporting rails inclined upwards to the water's edge. Her colleagues in the Industry Section told her that it had been pigeon-holed long ago as something to do with land reclamation, but she was not convinced.

When Kendall returned late that afternoon from his meeting in London, he found awaiting him a message to the effect that Section Officer Babington Smith would like to see him. He seemed to her a little pale and tired when he entered her office, but clearly his faith in his hunch was as firm as ever. When she offered her rather diffident suggestion that the ramp she showed him might be a catapult for pilotless aircraft, he said confidently that he *knew* it was.

She understood why when, still later that afternoon, she had her first sight of the photographs brought back by Merifield on November 28. Only one photograph, taken right at the beginning of the run, showed her ramp. But that one was plenty. For there, on the ramp, was one of the tiny aircraft which she had first spotted on November 13 and had called the Peenemünde 20.

On the same day, almost at the very moment when Constance Babington Smith was poring over the photographs which showed her ramp and wondering what it was, interpreters searching Merifield's cover of Zinnowitz for the suspected radar installation found, in wooded country eight miles south-east of Peenemünde, ramps built on foundations which matched the rectangular concrete slabs at the ski sites. So the search was over. The flying bomb, hitherto masquerading as the Peenemünde 20, had been tracked down. The link between Zinnowitz and Bois Carré was firm. The ski sites were for flying bombs. The curved buildings were obviously for storing components of the missile with some protection against blast. The square building must be, as indeed it was, for setting a magnetic compass.

These discoveries were hailed as a triumph for photographic reconnaissance, and so they were. They were also a triumph for a diverse team of investigators, most of whom saw only a small part of the game and were sometimes inclined to scoff at the activities of unknown collaborators whose corner of the field was not theirs. Reconnaissance pilots and photographic interpreters smiled at the cloak-and-dagger boys who came forward with their blithe demands for news of a radar mast in a German forest five hundred miles away. Yet, without the cloak-and-dagger boys, the ski sites would never have been discovered except by a fluke, no one would ever have heard of Zinnowitz, and in all probability Peenemünde would have attracted no more attention from the Photographic Reconnaissance Unit and the Central Interpretation Unit in 1943 than it received during the first three years of the war.

II

The discovery that the Peenemünde 20 was a flying bomb, and

that there were ramps at Zinnowitz and Peenemünde which explained the purpose of the ski sites, brought home to the authorities in Britain the existence of a threat which seemed to some of them even more formidable than in fact it was. There were nearly a hundred ski sites, and the curved buildings were estimated to provide storage space for the components of twenty missiles at each site. On the assumption that stocks would be replenished daily, it was natural to conclude that a scale of attack of the order of two thousand missiles a day might be expected if the Germans were left to complete their programme without interference.

In reality the outlook in December, although grave enough, was not quite so alarming. If the ski sites had been completed the Germans would have ninety-six of them, in addition to the three 'protected' launching-sites at Lottinghem, Siracourt and Equeurdreville; but they were not planning to use all their sites at once. The launching-regiment consisted of eight supply and maintenance batteries and sixteen launching batteries, the last each capable of manning four positions. Thus the rate of fire, if the remaining British assumptions were sound, might have amounted in theory to something like twelve hundred missiles a day.

Whether such a scale of attack could have been maintained in practice is another matter. Much heavier attacks than the Air Staff predicted were forecast in some quarters, but such estimates tended to ignore the human factor.* According to German calculations, the launching of two missiles an hour from each of sixty-four sites for an average of ten hours a day ought not to have been beyond the regiment's capabilities. But to keep up an offensive at that rate for any length of time would have meant bringing to the forward area every week not only more than eight thousand missiles, each taking about two hundred and eighty man-hours to produce, but also about a

* See, for example, pp. 60–61.

million gallons of low-octane aviation spirit for the missiles themselves and substantial quantities of hydrogen peroxide and permanganate of potash for the catapults which shot them from the ramps. That the German production and transportation systems could have performed such feats seems improbable in the light of their subsequent achievements.

Even so, the ski sites would certainly have been capable of an offensive which might have done great harm. Recognising that prompt action was needed to knock them out, the authorities took it. Wing Commander Kendall's report emphasising the significance of the finds at Zinnowitz and Peenemünde was written during the night of December 1, and reached Whitehall early on December 2. On December 4 fresh cover of the whole of Northern France within 140 miles of London or Portsmouth was ordered as an insurance against the risk that some sites might not have been reported by agents and might therefore have been overlooked when previous cover was laid on. In the meantime recent cover of the ninety-five sites identified made it possible to prepare and distribute target-material with great speed. On December 5 attacks on known sites were begun by fighter-bombers and light bombers of the Second Tactical Air Force and the United States Ninth Air Force.

Calculating that a ski site could be constructed from start to finish in six weeks, the experts soon saw, however, that such attacks as the tactical air forces could expect to deliver on the relatively few days when circumstances were favourable would not be enough to prevent the Germans from completing a high proportion of sites during the winter months if they gave their minds to it. Nor was the weather often suitable for night attacks by the British Bomber Command. After high-level discussion a heavy attack by day bombers of the United States Eighth Air Force on as many sites as possible was arranged for Christmas Eve, when 672 Fortresses aimed 1,472 tons of bombs at 24 sites. Neither Air Chief Marshal Harris of Bomber Command nor

Lieutenant-General Carl Spaatz, commanding the United States Strategic Air Forces in Europe, liked to see the heavy bomber forces diverted from their appointed task of wearing down German industry and the spirits of the German people; but the British Chiefs of Staff attached so much importance to the destruction of the ski sites and 'large sites' that in April they exercised their right to appeal to the Supreme Commander if they thought that their requirements for the security of the United Kingdom were not being fully met. General Eisenhower promised that everything possible should be done to secure the safety of the British Isles as a base for operations against Germany, and thereafter both the tactical air forces and the United States Eighth Air Force notably increased their scale of attack.

In the outcome, the two tactical air forces and the two heavy bomber forces aimed more than three thousand tons of bombs at the ski sites between December 5 and the end of the year, and a further twenty thousand tons between January 1 and June 12, 1944. In addition more than eight thousand tons were aimed at the 'large sites', chiefly because they were suspected of a connection with the long-range rocket. The grand total of thirty-one thousand tons was more than half as large again as the whole weight of bombs (about nineteen thousand tons) which the Germans had aimed at London in major attacks during the eight months of the 'Blitz' from September, 1940, to May, 1941.

British experts estimated early in 1944 that twenty-one of the fifty-two ski sites attacked up to the end of 1943 had been heavily damaged or virtually destroyed. Another fifteen, they thought, had probably sustained some damage. Noticing that, where the Germans repaired the sites, they paid most attention to the launching-platform and the square building, they concluded that these were the essential features. In June, after another five months' bombing, the Air Staff estimated, rather hopefully, that an effort equivalent to that of eight completed sites might be expected from the remaining ski sites if the Germans decided to use them for an improvised offensive.

According to German records, Allied air attacks destroyed only seven of the sites in December, 1943. The effect was nevertheless decisive. Almost irrespective of the damage done, the attacks gave General Heinemann the best of reasons for believing that his distrust of the ski sites was well founded, that there was no chance of mounting a successful offensive from them, and that he would have to make a fresh start with sites less conspicuous and less vulnerable.

If the British search for the flying bomb reached a climax with the discovery of the nature of the ski sites and the decision to bomb them, the period that followed was one of anti-climax. When Heinemann obtained the approval of his superiors for a new programme of site-construction, he took care that it was carried out by men who understood the virtues of concealment. Constructional work was reduced to the bare minimum. The curved buildings were omitted, apparently on the argument that, if piloted aircraft could be dispersed in the open, as they were at well-regulated Royal Air Force and Luftwaffe bases, then the components of pilotless aircraft could quite well be dispersed in woods. At most of the new sites only the concrete floors of the launching-ramp and the square building were laid, leaving the structures to be completed at the last moment with pre-fabricated parts delivered in a form suitable for final assembly on the spot. At one or two sites where the square building was completed at an earlier stage, it was heavily camouflaged.

At the same time, security was tightened up. Some of the precautions taken seemed theatrical, but they served their purpose. When a newcomer with a name which had not hitherto figured in the German military hierarchy made his appearance as alleged commander of the launching-units in France,

Allied intelligence officers were bound to take some time to discover that he was merely their old friend Colonel Wachtel wearing a pseudonym and otherwise disguised. Headquarters were changed, leave was restricted, letters home were heavily censored or forbidden. French labour was intentionally mis-employed on ski sites which had ceased to matter. Redoubling their vigilance, German counter-agents succeeded in pene-trating part of the French resistance movement, with the result that Allied agents were caught, material intended only for Allied eyes was captured, and opportunities were created for the Germans to sow misleading reports.

In consequence, Allied intelligence was not so prompt to plumb the mysteries of the new 'modified' sites as to plumb those of the ski sites. Information about the new sites began to reach London in February, but it lacked the precision which enabled photographic interpreters to locate the first of the ski sites at Bois Carré, and afterwards go on to locate the rest. The modified sites were much less conspicuous than the ski sites. Even so, there could scarcely be a more convincing demonstra-tion of the difficulty of photographic reconnaissance and inter-pretation without a lead from other sources than the failure of the Allies to locate the first of the modified sites until April 27, some three months after their construction began and many weeks after their existence was first vaguely reported. Captain Robert Rowell of the Central Interpretation Unit then spotted on photographs taken near Cherbourg a site at Bel-hamelin which reproduced the essential features of the ski sites, but had no curved buildings.

During the next fortnight another nineteen modified sites were discovered, and by early June the total rose to sixty-six (or sixty-four according to another source). This was a good deal less than half the number of sites planned, and substantially less than the number virtually ready, so far as constructional work was concerned, in the area north and east of the Seine alone.

The Allied landing in Normandy was thus only a few weeks away by the time intelligence officers had located enough sites to make out a case for attacking them, and the great air offensive which was to pave the way for the landing was in full swing. Their chances of persuading their superiors to divert part of the Allied bomber effort to the sites were therefore not as good as they might have been if the sites had been discovered earlier. The modified sites, with hardly anything showing above ground, were not attractive targets from the physical point of view, but the psychological factor was also important. By the middle of May air supremacy over Northern France was such a glittering prospect that there was a tendency in high circles to brush aside anything that marred the perfection of the picture. Too readily assuming that the bombing of the ski sites had scotched the menace of the flying bomb, some senior officers and their staffs showed little inclination to be bothered with the new bogy of the modified sites which the prophets of woe had tardily coaxed out of its lair. Moreover, even those who did pause to weigh the significance of the new sites were confident that the addition of launching-rails and other finishing touches would give them all the warning they needed if and when the sites were made ready for use. A qualifying clause overlooked by some was that this would be true only if the intelligence staffs could count on knowing in good time that the finishing touches had been made. Not everyone foresaw that far-reaching demands on the reconnaissance squadrons while the Allies were going ashore would leave photographic interpreters dependent on chance cover of the sites at a crucial time, and hence more than ever at the mercy of the weather.

The consequence was that no attempt was made to bomb the modified sites apart from one experimental attack by fighter-bombers on May 27. In a memorandum circulated on Sunday, June 11, the Air Staff committed themselves to the opinion that the modified sites were unlikely to be fit for use 'on any appreciable scale' within the next few weeks, and that probably the worst that need be feared in the immediate future was that a few ski sites might go into action.

Fortunately for their reputation, this was not their last word on the subject before the Germans opened their attack. Too late on June 10 for them to alter their memorandum, a report reached London from a Belgian source to the effect that a goods trains carrying nearly a hundred large objects described as rockets had passed through Ghent in the direction of the Franco-Belgian frontier. Rapid confirmation of a suspicion that these were really flying bombs without their wings was received when on June 11 nine modified sites were photographed after a lapse of six days during which no cover had been possible. At six of the sites 'much activity' was visible, at four of them rails had been laid on the ramps, and at six the square building had been completed. Next morning, some eighteen hours before the first flying bomb reached the United Kingdom, Air Vice-Marshal F. F. Inglis, Assistant Chief of the Air Staff (Intelligence), warned the Chiefs of Staff that the Germans seemed to be making 'energetic preparations to bring the pilotless aircraft sites into operation at an early date'.

4

The Advance to Contact : Defence

WHEN the Chiefs of Staff decided early in December, 1943, that the ski sites should be bombed, they also decided that the time had come when the air defences must get ready to shoot down such pilotless aircraft as the enemy might still be able to send across the Channel after the Allied air forces had done their worst.

At that time a substantial part of the Allied war-machine had just assumed a new shape in preparation for the landing in Normandy which was due in the late spring or early summer. On November 15, 1943, Fighter Command was temporarily renamed Air Defence of Great Britain and put under the Allied Expeditionary Air Force, which in turn was part of the Allied Expeditionary Force under the Supreme Commander. These changes were followed by a marked shrinkage of the resources available to the air defence commander, but they did not bring any corresponding reduction of his defensive commitments. No longer a Commander-in-Chief but henceforth a mere Air Marshal Commanding, he was still the man immediately responsible for defending the United Kingdom against all forms of air attack. He retained control not only of the fighter and balloon-barrage squadrons which he commanded through his own subordinate formations, but also of the anti-aircraft artillery and searchlight formations administered by the War Office through Anti-Aircraft Command.

In addition the air defence commander would be responsible,

THE AIR DEFENCES OF THE UNITED KINGDOM AND THEIR RELATION TO THE SUPREME ALLIED COMMAND: SUMMER, 1944

This diagram shows the chain of command reduced to its simplest terms. Names of commanders mentioned in the text are in heavy type.

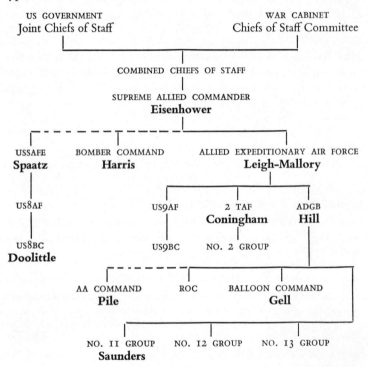

Abbreviations

USSAFE — United States Strategic Air Forces in Europe.

US8AF — United States 8th Air Force.

US9AF — United States 9th Air Force.

2 TAF — Second Tactical Air Force.

ADGB — Air Defence of Great Britain.

US8BC — United States 8th Bomber Command.

US9BC — United States 9th Bomber Command.

ROC — Royal Observer Corps.

during the assault phase of the landing in Normandy, for the air defence of the lodgement area between dusk and dawn. For the time being he was charged also, at least in theory, with the conduct of certain offensive operations involving both his own squadrons and British fighter-bomber and tactical bomber squadrons. In practice the tactical co-ordination of these operations was done by the Air Officer Commanding No. 11 Group, who was the air defence commander's subordinate but dealt directly with the Allied Expeditionary Force or the Second Tactical Air Force where offensive operations were in view.

The new post of Air Marshal Commanding, Air Defence of Great Britain, went to Air Marshal R. M. (afterwards Sir Roderic) Hill. The Allied Expeditionary Air Force was commanded by Air Chief Marshal Sir Trafford Leigh-Mallory, who thus became ultimately responsible, at least in theory, for Hill's work. Air Chief Marshal Sir Arthur Tedder, the Deputy Supreme Commander of the Allied Expeditionary Force, had a special though rather indeterminate responsibility where air matters were concerned, and was senior to Leigh-Mallory. Air Marshal Sir Arthur Coningham commanded the Second Tactical Air Force, which formed part of Leigh-Mallory's resources.

Unlike Coningham, whose reputation had been won in the Mediterranean theatre, both Leigh-Mallory and Hill had gained much of their experience as group commanders in Fighter Command. As commander of No. 12 Group in 1940, Leigh-Mallory had attracted notice by lending support to criticisms of his neighbour at No. 11 Group, Air Vice-Marshal Park, who was accused in some quarters of using his squadrons in penny numbers. Notwithstanding Park's tactical success in the Battle of Britain, Leigh-Mallory was brought in to replace him soon after Air Marshal W. S. Douglas (afterwards Lord Douglas of Kirtleside) succeeded Air Chief Marshal Dowding as Commander-in-Chief. Leigh-Mallory in turn drew fire from the critics by incurring rather heavy losses in the offensive operations which he favoured, but went on to succeed Douglas before becoming Allied Air Commander. A poor pilot but a keen student of air strategy, he was a short, energetic, lively-minded man, with a confident way of expressing himself which irritated some people and convinced others that his understanding of the problems of air power was wide and deep. Often accused by his enemies of vanity and boastfulness, he was well liked by those among his staff who knew him best.

Hill won neither fame nor notoriety when he, too, commanded a fighter group, but had already gained a reputation as one of the ablest pilots of single-seater machines the Royal Air Force ever had. His background and tastes were scholarly. He was fond of music, wrote well and drew competently but without inspiration. In his youth he was known as a brilliant yet level-headed manipulator of aircraft to whom the first trial of a new technique could safely be entrusted in the knowledge that he understood the risks involved and had weighed the prospects of success and failure. In his early fifties he could hold his own with men half his age at the controls of the latest and fastest fighters. Tall, good-looking and unfailingly polite, he stemmed from the Cambridge tradition of experimental philosophers for whom successful action is the correct application of sound principles. Gaiety, courage, devotion to duty and an absorbing interest in the job in hand were all comprehended in his definition of the correct.

On paper, the arrangements which came into force in November, 1943, made Hill a subordinate commander, responsible to Leigh-Mallory, who in turn was answerable to the Supreme Commander and the Chiefs of Staff for the safety of the United Kingdom in face of air attack. In practice, they did not have quite that effect. Leigh-Mallory's interests were pre-eminently offensive. He was preoccupied with the air assault which paved the way for the landings in Normandy, and later with the air aspect of the break-out and the push towards the Rhine. He kept a tight hold on certain administrative questions which affected the air defences, and in the early stages also on offensive operations in which defensive fighters shared; in other respects he gave Hill virtually a free hand. Once the Allied armies were established on French soil, an increasing proportion of Leigh-Mallory's time was spent on the Continent. Hill was therefore obliged to deal directly with the Air Ministry, the Chiefs of Staff, and other high-level bodies.

This had its advantages for Hill, but it also had its drawbacks. So far as defensive operations were concerned, the burden of command and staff work was always bound to fall on him and his subordinates, not only because that was the arrangement contemplated in the new deal, but also because Leigh-Mallory was not much interested in pure defence and because his Anglo-American staff lacked corporate experience of defensive problems. What can scarcely have been contemplated was that Hill should have practically all the responsibilities of a Commander-in-Chief without the status of one. Nominally, Leigh-Mallory was the man whom the Air Staff were supposed to blame if air defence matters did not go according to their liking; in practice, Leigh-Mallory's voluntary dissociation from the defensive side of his huge job made it fairly certain that they would blame Hill.

At the same time, Hill was the first air defence commander who was called upon to exercise operational control of the guns and searchlights from a subordinate position. A youngish, newly-promoted Air Marshal, scarcely known outside his own service, he had the delicate task of imposing his wishes on a very senior Lieutenant-General of the British Army. Lieutenant-General Sir Frederick Pile had headed Anti-Aircraft Command since before the outbreak of war, was considerably older and more experienced than Hill, and was well known to the Prime

Minister and other members of the government. If relations between the two men were uniformly good, it was because Hill was tactful and because Pile, an Irish baronet, son of a former Lord Mayor of Dublin and a man mellowed by wide knowledge of the world, had always been more interested in helping air defence commanders to do a good job than in standing on his dignity. But that did not save Hill from being unjustly suspected of giving undue weight to Pile's views.

In December the Air Staff, prompted by the Chiefs of Staff, ordered Leigh-Mallory to 'consider, in consultation with the G.O.C.-in-C., Anti-Aircraft Command' what counter-measures to pilotless aircraft were possible with the resources at his disposal and draw up plans accordingly. So far as defensive counter-measures were concerned, Leigh-Mallory delegated the task to Hill. He also passed on an 'appreciation' in which the Air Staff estimated the speed of the missile at anything from 250 to 420 miles an hour and added that it might fly at any altitude between 500 and 7,000 feet. The air defences were to be ready by February, 1944, to meet attacks at the rate of two missiles an hour from each of a hundred launching-sites.

Pointing out that these estimates were so broad as to make detailed planning difficult, Hill asked for something more specific. Thus pressed, the Air Staff committed themselves, with reservations, to the opinion that 400 miles an hour was a likely average speed, and raised their estimate of the missile's probable altitude to 7,500 feet. Later they reduced their figures for speed and height to 350 miles an hour and 7,000 feet, and still later to 330 miles an hour and 6,000 feet. They also revised their forecasts of the date and scale of attack as offensive counter-measures got under way and as more and more of the ski sites were thought to have been knocked out or badly damaged.

Meanwhile Hill had come to the conclusion that the missiles, even if they flew too fast to be caught by the fighters on which the air defences had relied in the past, would be vulnerable, in principle, to the same methods as were used against piloted aircraft. In an outline plan which he submitted to Leigh-Mallory on December 16, he proposed that anti-aircraft guns, searchlights, balloons and fighters should all be tried, but urged that the bombing of ski sites should be continued with the utmost vigour for fear his fighters might prove too slow.

Hill also asked to be kept informed of the fate of proposals to divert the missiles either by radio interference or by electromagnetic means. The first of these proposals came to nothing when it was found that the missiles were not controlled by radio, the second when calculation showed that creation of the required magnetic field would consume such vast quantities of copper wire and electric power that the project was not feasible.

On January 2, 1944, Hill followed with a detailed plan. On receiving warning of an imminent attack, fighters would patrol at 12,000 feet twenty miles off the coast between Beachy Head and the South Foreland, over the coast between Newhaven and Dover, and over Kent and Sussex between Haywards Heath and Ashford. Other fighters would patrol the same lines at 6,000 feet when the missiles began to arrive. In addition, Hill and Pile proposed to deploy 400 heavy and 346 light anti-aircraft guns and 216 searchlights immediately south of London; a further 96 heavy and 216 light guns and 132 searchlights near Bristol, which was threatened by some sites near Cherbourg; and 32 heavy and 242 light guns, with a smaller number of searchlights, round the Solent, where there were several likely targets. As a further line of defence for London, 480 barrage balloons would fly at all hours of the day and night above the belt of high ground between Cobham, Kent and Limpsfield, Surrey. As Hill intended to thin out the balloon defences in any case, he would be able to find that number of balloons without reducing any existing barrages below the strength he already meant to give them.

About three weeks after receiving these proposals, the Chiefs of Staff came to the conclusion that attacks with pilotless aircraft were not likely to begin before March 1, and later they decided that March 15 was the earliest date by which the Germans could be ready. As preparations for the landing in Normandy were due to begin in earnest on April 1, the result was that early in February Hill faced a new demand for a truncated plan which could be reconciled with the needs of the invasion forces. He and Pile succeeded, however, in getting authority to make certain administrative arrangements on the assumption that their original plan might have to be put into effect.

At the time when Hill and Pile were called upon for a new version of their plan, attacks on the ski sites were believed to be going well, and the menace of the 'modified' sites was not yet apparent. Accordingly, they were not required to provide against more than the relatively light scale of attack expected from such ski sites as might survive the bombing, or to earmark more resources than could safely be set aside without detriment to offensive operations. With these restrictions in mind, they reduced their special allotment of heavy and light guns to the London area to 192 and 246 respectively, left the allotment of heavy guns to Bristol as it was but reduced the number of light guns to 36, and decided that no special provision need be made for the Solent in view of the substantial number of guns which would be deployed there in any case while the invasion forces were assembling. Fifty-four of the light guns allotted to the London defences, and all the heavy and light guns allotted to Bristol, would be released for other work by the time the Allies went ashore in Normandy, so that altogether 240 heavy and 522 light guns would be saved up to that time, and a further 96 heavy and 90 light guns thereafter. A substantial number of searchlights could be saved, too, by reducing or abolishing special allotments and relying wholly or partly on the ordinary anti-aircraft layout in some areas. On the other hand, there was no need to reduce the allotment to the special balloon barrage, since the balloons were not needed for other purposes.

Hill submitted the new plan to Leigh-Mallory towards the end of February, after first making sure that Pile and his staff had so framed their part of it as to allow the number of guns to be increased without much difficulty if the need arose and if more guns could be found. He also took the precaution of pointing out that the gunners would face a particularly awkward task if the missiles should happen to fly at 2,000 to 3,000 feet instead of the 6,000 feet predicted by the Air Staff; for they would then be too high for the light guns and too low for the heavies. Leigh-Mallory approved the plan, so did the Supreme Commander and the Chiefs of Staff, and on March 4 Hill sent copies of it to formations which would have to act on it if it ever went into force.

Thus it was with the new plan in their files that commanders and staff officers who would have to deal with the missiles if they crossed the Channel waited through the weeks that followed for the enemy to show his hand. March passed, and with it the date by which Hill had been told to expect that the threat, already deferred more than once since he received his first warning in the early winter, might materialise at any moment. So did April. Nothing happened, except that more attacks were made on ski sites and that more damage to them was reported and duly catalogued by Hill's staff.

May and the early part of June passed, too, but with a difference. The end of April brought the discovery of the Bel-hamelin site. In due course the news reached Hill's headquarters at Stanmore and the headquarters of the Allied Expeditionary Air Force close by. Soon more sites of the same type were discovered. By the middle of May there was a growing list of new, easily-constructed launching-sites which seemed to intelligence officers to cry out for attack. But Hill's officers found when they discussed the significance of the 'modified' sites with their opposite numbers across the way that Leigh-Mallory's staff were not much interested. Men who had helped to kindle the flame of life at Leigh-Mallory's headquarters and had taught some of his officers all they knew about the flying bomb were told in rather chilling terms that the Allied Expeditionary Air Force attached little importance to the new sites.

Many reasons were afterwards given for the failure of the Allied air forces to attack the 'modified' sites in May and early June. The sites made poor targets, they were hard for aircrew to spot, and so on. All these were good reasons so far as they went, but they were in the nature of excuses. The inescapable truth was that Leigh-Mallory had little attention to spare for the new sites. He was wrapped up in the problem of how the Allies could best use their immense air power to put their armies safely ashore in Normandy and help them to consolidate their foothold. His staff, on their own showing, took the threat from the 'modified' sites too lightly, and could plead in extenuation that the Air Staff at the Air Ministry also did so until the eleventh hour. The shortcomings of the new sites as bombing targets would not have prevented the Allies from attacking them if everyone concerned had been alive to the danger they presented.

As things were, the notion that the 'modified' sites were much less formidable than the ski sites was so deeply rooted that some senior officers clung to it even when the war was over. Marshal of the Royal Air Force Sir Arthur Harris asserted after the war that at one time the Germans planned to launch six thousand flying bombs a day from sixty-four sites, and that the bombing of the ski sites forced them to use 'a much less efficient type of site'.* His deputy, Air Marshal Sir Robert Saundby, added that the 'modified' sites could launch only two missiles an hour instead of the 'hundreds a day' which the

* Marshal of the R.A.F. Sir Arthur Harris, *Bomber Offensive* (1947), pp. 198 and 216.

ski sites were designed to launch.* These distinguished officers were not alone in assuming that the ski sites were capable of a very much higher rate of fire than was ever achieved by the 'modified' sites or expected of them. The fallacy behind that assumption becomes apparent when one reflects that the Germans had only sixty-four launching-teams and eight supply and maintenance batteries, that storing the missiles in curved buildings instead of dispersing them in woods would not have turned the rank-and-file into supermen, and that there was only one square building at each site. A daily effort of six thousand missiles would have meant the launching by each team of an average of one missile every sixteen minutes for twenty-four hours a day. Every sixteen minutes, all round the clock, the men at each site would have had to trundle a missile to the square building, fit wings to it, set the compass, pump the best part of a hundred and fifty gallons of fuel into it, and remove it to a freshly-prepared launching-ramp while another missile took its place. Where jams and hitches were always likely, such feats were out of the question even if the forty thousand missiles and five or six million gallons of fuel needed every week could have been provided.

Nor can it even be assumed that the bombing of the ski sites delayed the start of the German offensive for more than a few weeks, if at all. The bombing had barely got into its stride when General Heinemann foresaw that technical shortcomings and production hold-ups would put active operations out of court until the following May or June at the earliest. In the outcome, the offensive did begin in June. If Heinemann was right, the bombing of Kassel would seem to have done at least as much to prevent an earlier start as the bombing of the ski sites. Allied bombing also helped to hamper Heinemann and his subordinate commanders immediately before and after the V.1 offensive began, by making the passage of the missiles to the forward

* Air Marshal Sir Robert Saundby, *Air Bombardment* (1961), p. 190.

area more difficult, although that was only a by-product of the attacks on French rail-centres which the Allies delivered as part of their invasion plan. But there is no reason to suppose that the Germans would not have been equally hampered in that way if they had stuck to their original intention and used the ski sites. Indeed, they might have been still worse off if they had done so than they were as things turned out, since the system of supply which they contemplated using when an offensive from the ski sites was in prospect was even more vulnerable to bombing than the system they did use.

5

The Advance to Contact : Attack

I

THE chain of command of the German organisation for long-range bombardment of the United Kingdom, which took shape between September, 1943, and the end of the year, was based on the assumption that simultaneous offensives with both the flying bomb and the A-4 rocket would begin in the early winter. That was not a realistic assumption by the time the scheme was sanctioned, but it nevertheless conditioned the thinking of planners apparently unaware of the technical hitches and production difficulties which made it untenable. One consequence was a top-heaviness which gave the German security organisation an unexpected bonus. Allied intelligence officers who knew that the rocket-launching troops had been commanded since the autumn of 1943 by a Major-General answerable to a corps commander and that there was also a flying bomb regiment commanded by a Colonel were puzzled when they failed to find enough troops to account for so much brass. The explanation was, of course, that recruitment and training on the A-4 side were much behind the high-level organisation.

The scheme drawn up in 1943 allotted responsibility for carrying out both offensives to LXV Armee Korps, a corps formed specially for the purpose under General Heinemann. Heinemann's command consisted of Colonel Wachtel's Flakregiment 155 (W), with its sixteen launching-batteries and eight supply and maintenance batteries concerned with the flying bomb, and the parallel organisation concerned with the long-range rocket. At first designated ARKO (Artillery Commander) 91, the chief post in the rocket-launching organisation was renamed HARKO (Senior Artillery Commander) 91 shortly before General Metz replaced General Dornberger as its holder, leaving Dornberger to concentrate on technical development and training. Much as Wachtel's troops were organised in four brigades and were expected to man sixty-four positions chosen from the ninety-six sites of Bois Carré type prepared for them between the Pas de Calais and Cherbourg and from the 'large sites' at Lottinghem, Siracourt and Equeurdreville, so Metz's were also organised in four brigades of which three were mobile and one was static. With the help of an independent battery to be formed by the SS, these formations were due to man thirty-nine groups of launching-platforms north of the Somme and six in Western Normandy, as well as the 'large sites' at Wizernes and Sottevast.

By early December, when Heinemann took up his post, it must have been obvious to anyone in touch with informed technical opinion at Peenemünde and in Berlin that these expectations were not likely to be fulfilled before the following summer and might never be fulfilled at all. As an experienced artillery commander, Heinemann had learnt to distrust innovators who claimed revolutionary advances; but he did not need to be specially sceptical to know that only ignorance of the facts or wishful thinking could lead the High Command to suppose that a two-pronged offensive might begin before the end of the year or early in 1944. Apart from the comparative ease with which the Bois Carré sites and the 'large' sites could be destroyed or isolated by Allied bombing, neither the rocket nor the bomb was anything like ready for use in substantial numbers. Since Bomber Command's raid on Peenemünde in August, many tests of the rocket had been made at Blizna, where the missiles did not have to be aimed out to sea but could

THE GERMAN LONG-RANGE BOMBARDMENT
ORGANISATION

The diagram shows the organisation and chain of command projected in the early part of 1944, on the assumption that four
Abteilungen and an independent battery would be available for
active operations with the A-4 rocket.

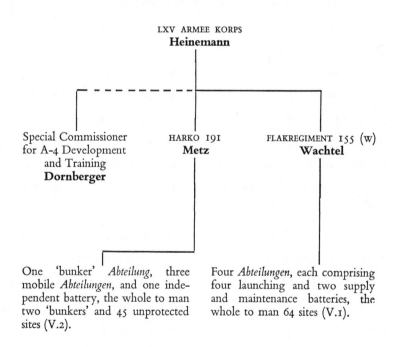

LXV ARMEE KORPS
Heinemann

Special Commissioner
for A-4 Development
and Training
Dornberger

HARKO 191
Metz

FLAKREGIMENT 155 (W)
Wachtel

One 'bunker' *Abteilung*, three
mobile *Abteilungen*, and one independent battery, the whole to man
two 'bunkers' and 45 unprotected
sites (V.2).

Four *Abteilungen*, each comprising
four launching and two supply
and maintenance batteries, the
whole to man 64 sites (V.1).

be fired across Polish territory. These tests showed not only that fewer than half the launchings were successful, but also that most of the rockets successfully launched fell to pieces before they reached the target. As for the bomb, production had barely got into its stride after a late start in September. Moreover, although the fact may not have been fully apparent as early as December, the bombs made at Fallersleben did not fly as fast as trials of prototypes and limited-production models had led the experts to expect. Dr Gosslau of Argus Motorenwerke explained after the war that this shortcoming could easily have been put right if he had not been refused permission to make the simple adjustment needed. Apparently the authorities were afraid that any tinkering might bring fresh delays; but another motive which seems to have weighed with them was that, by the time the weapon was ready for use, there was a case for encouraging the Allies to keep a fair proportion of their anti-aircraft defences in England by sending them a missile capable of doing a good deal of damage but which they had a sporting chance of bringing down.

The sequel was the decision to abandon the Bois Carré sites, accompanied by Heinemann's prediction that an offensive with the bomb alone might be possible in the following May or June. Series production of the rocket at Niedersachswerfen began in January, 1944, but was soon suspended to give Dornberger a chance of improving the design, since there seemed to be no point in turning out missiles of which the greater part were destined to disintegrate in the air if they ever got off the ground. During the next few months he and his technicians succeeded, by empirical methods, in greatly reducing the proportion of rockets which broke up before they reached the target, although they did not get to the bottom of the trouble until later. To give the war-head a better chance of reaching the neighbourhood of the target before exploding when the rocket did break up in the air, arrangements were made to fit a relatively insensitive fuse at the cost of making the explosion rather less effective.

As a logical corollary to Heinemann's forecast that the bomb, but not the rocket, might be ready by May or June, preparations for an offensive from Northern France by Wachtel's troops were a good deal more realistic than preparations for an accompanying offensive by Metz's. By the early summer an elaborate plan for the launching of rockets from the forty-five groups of platforms and two 'large sites' allotted to Metz reposed in the files of Heinemann's headquarters near Paris, but whether it would ever be translated into action was another matter. If it were, the missiles would be stored at seven main depots in various parts of France and Belgium, and distributed through four field storage depots and six transit dumps in forward areas. Launching-units would draw their liquid oxygen from bulk stores in the Pas de Calais and Calvados, their alcohol from eight forward depots replenished from reserves near Lille and in the suburbs of Paris. Heinemann's policy seems to have been to allow these preparations to go forward on the principle that readiness for all contingencies could do no harm, and that there was always an outside chance that Dornberger and his friends might be able to produce the rocket in time for him to use it before the long-threatened Allied landing in Northern France put the project out of court. At the same time, he can hardly have failed to be aware that the system of supply would be hard to conceal from Allied agents once it was in use, and that its dependence on railways and roads within easy reach of British and American bombers would make it highly vulnerable.

Conversely, great pains were taken to make Wachtel's lines of communication as safe as possible, although they too depended on French and Belgian roads and railways. Up to the early part of 1944 the plan was that his launching-teams should receive supplies from three depots north of the Somme, three between the Somme and the Seine, and two in Normandy west of the Seine. All eight were served by rail spurs, and all, as Heinemann had good reason to guess, were duly spotted by Allied intelligence officers, who listed them as 'supply sites' although they were not sure of their connection with the flying bomb. In view of Heinemann's concern with security it is not surprising that the Germans, when they rejected the Bois Carré launching-sites with their distinctive ski-shaped buildings, also abandoned the eight supply sites, whose place in the system was taken by two large limestone caverns at Nucourt and Saint-Leu-d'Esserent, in the valley of the Oise, and a railway tunnel at Rilly-la-Montagne, south of Rheims.

Between the beginning of 1944 and the middle of the second week in June, Heinemann had the satisfaction of seeing the Allies expend thousands of tons of bombs on the abandoned 'ski' sites and the almost equally useless 'large sites', while Wachtel's 'modified' sites and the new storage depots at Nucourt, Saint-Leu-d'Esserent and Rilly-la-Montagne went unscathed. The one experimental attack made on a 'modified' site by fighter-bombers had no practical effect, although it must have caused Heinemann and Wachtel at least a momentary qualm. As for the system of supply, Allied intelligence officers pointed out when the 'modified' launching-sites of Belhamelin type made their appearance that the role of the constructions which they called supply sites had become more problematical than ever. To test the enemy's response, United States bombers twice attacked a selected supply site at Beauvoir, in Western Normandy, dropping nearly three hundred tons of bombs and cutting the rail spur which served the site. These blows inflicted no hardship on the Germans, who gave the Allies an interesting pointer by doing nothing to restore communications for at least twelve days.

II

Early on June 6 the Allies landed in Western Normandy under cover of a stratagem which gave the impression that their main effort would be made in the Pas de Calais or astride the Somme. A few hours later Wachtel received orders from Heinemann to prepare for an immediate offensive against the United Kingdom. In spite of Allied bombing of French communication centres, which caused considerable difficulties and almost halted rail traffic by day, 873 flying bombs were distributed to launching-teams from the depots at Nucourt and Saint-Leu-d'Esserent within six days, and large quantities of aviation spirit and other fuels were delivered. By the evening of June 12, launching-rails were in position at fifty-four or fifty-five of the seventy to eighty virtually completed sites north and east of the Seine.

Heinemann's authority for the orders he gave Wachtel on June 6 must have come from a high quarter. Such a departure was not likely to be sanctioned without the Führer's express approval, but whether Hitler initiated the move or merely agreed to it is not clear. After the German Army had failed to prevent the Allies from getting a foothold in Normandy, he countered defeatist talk among senior officers by asserting that an offensive with flying bombs would force the Allies to rush their reserves to the Pas de Calais in the hope of capturing the launching-sites, the implication being that this would give Rommel's armour a chance of meeting the enemy on favourable terms. When Wachtel received his orders on June 6, however, the situation was still so fluid that the Supreme Command can hardly have assumed that their attempt to push the Allies back into the sea in Normandy was bound to fail, or that any inducement from Wachtel was needed to precipitate the further landings in the Pas de Calais which they expected almost hourly on that day and for some days afterwards. Thus Hitler's subsequent remarks to disconsolate generals are not reliable evidence of his state of mind on June 6, although there is no reason to doubt the genuineness of his belief that Wachtel's offensive might have the effect suggested. A feeling that all parts of Northern France from which flying bombs or long-range rockets might be launched ought to be mopped up did, in fact, play some part in Allied strategic thinking after the break-out in August, but not earlier, when the eyes of those of the Allied leaders whose opinions mattered were firmly fixed on the all-important problems of building up the bridgehead, drawing Rommel's armour on to the British and Canadian fronts, and preparing for the great advance which carried the Allies to the Seine and over it.

An important conference to discuss the coming offensive was held on June 11 at Heinemann's headquarters at Maisons-Lafitte, on the Seine a few miles outside Paris. Colonel Walter, Heinemann's Chief of Staff, urged Wachtel to open his attack on the following day, but conceded that the bomb was an un-tried weapon so far as active operations went, and that the launching-teams would face conditions very different from those of the practice-ground at Zinnowitz, where experts were always at hand to overcome difficulties and answer questions. Astutely covering himself against a charge of excessive zeal, he added that his chief was quite ready to postpone the offensive if Wachtel was not satisfied that he had everything he needed. Wachtel pointed out that he was finding great difficulty in getting up supplies, that some of his units were still short of fuel, and that dummy missiles for practice shots were particularly scarce. In spite of Walter's disclaimer he can hardly have failed to suspect, however, that his superiors meant to press him to the limit and were not likely to look kindly on him if he did exercise his right to wait until his troops had their full quota of supplies. Finally he agreed that operations should begin on the evening of June 12, as Heinemann and Walter wished. The operational order from corps headquarters, which seems to have reached him on June 12, although he may have been shown the draft of it on the previous day, called on him to open with a salvo timed to reach London at 11.40 p.m. Thereafter 'harassing fire' was to continue until 4.45 a.m. on June 13, by which time about five hundred missiles would have been launched if Walter's expectations were fulfilled. This would mean a rate of fire of about two missiles an hour from each of the fifty to sixty sites expected to be in service.

Since the arrival of the warning order on June 6, Wachtel had moved from his headquarters near Beauvais to a command post at Saleux, near Amiens. It was therefore to Saleux that Heinemann, leaving Walter in charge at Maisons-Lafitte, went on the afternoon of June 12 with the object of lending moral support at a crucial stage. Perhaps fortunately for Wachtel, the corps commander was thus able to see for himself that firing a salvo of a novel kind from more than fifty inadequately-equipped positions, scattered over five thousand square miles of unfriendly territory dominated by a hostile air force, was not the straightforward job which Walter may have thought it.

For Wachtel's command post to keep in touch through brigade and battery headquarters with the launching-sites, most of them in out-of-the-way places where there were no telephones in peacetime, was itself no easy task at a time when communications tended to be interrupted by Allied bombing and the demands of urgent military traffic. Reports were, in fact, so slow in coming in that no comprehensive picture of the state of readiness of the sites was available until the time for action was perilously near. The situation then disclosed was so unsatisfactory that Wachtel must bitterly have regretted his surrender to Walter's plea for an immediate offensive. That, because of the shortage of dummy missiles, trial shots had been fired from only eighteen sites, so that the troops at the remain-

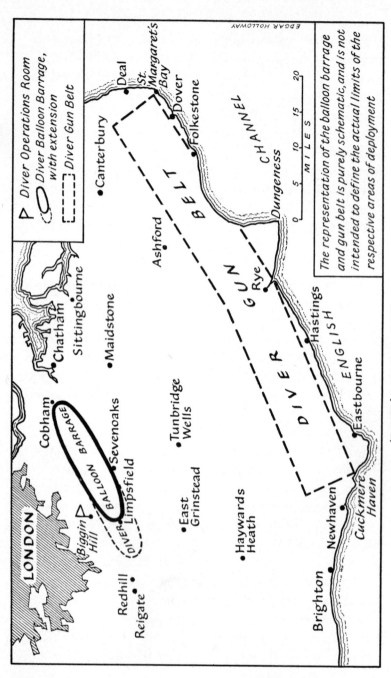

Legend:
- ▷ Diver Operations Room
- ⬭ Diver Balloon Barrage, with extension
- ▯▯▯ Diver Gun Belt

LONDON

Biggin Hill
Cobham
BALLOON BARRAGE
DIVER
Limpsfield
Sevenoaks
Redhill
Reigate
East Grinstead
Tunbridge Wells
Haywards Heath
Chatham
Sittingbourne
Maidstone
Canterbury
Deal
St. Margaret's Bay
Dover
Folkestone
Ashford
Dungeness
Rye
DIVER GUN BELT
Hastings
ENGLISH CHANNEL
Newhaven
Brighton
Eastbourne
Cuckmere Haven

0 5 10 15 20
MILES

The representation of the balloon barrage and gun belt is purely schematic, and is not intended to define the actual limits of the respective areas of deployment

EDGAR HOLLOWAY

'DIVER' LAYOUT: JULY 17, 1944

ing thirty-six or thirty-seven would be using their ramps and catapults for the first time when they went into action with live missiles, was bad enough; but it was not the worst. Literally at the eleventh hour Wachtel learned, apparently for the first time although it is hard to understand why so serious a shortcoming was not foreseen at the previous day's conference, that not one of his launching-teams was in a position to carry out the drill prescribed for a live shoot. Missiles were plentiful, enough fuel had been distributed to give every unit a chance of firing although not every one had its full quota; but at no site had the safety equipment which all teams were supposed to install before they fired yet arrived.

Apparently concluding that he could not expose two-thirds of his teams to the double hazard of untried ramps and no safety equipment, Wachtel decided to ask for an hour's grace. With the salvo due in London at twenty minutes before midnight, sites up to a hundred and thirty miles or more from the target would have to go into action about a quarter past eleven. By the time he had digested the last report and made up his mind what to do, he had less than fifteen minutes left in which to gain a respite.

The sequel throws an interesting sidelight on the respect paid to staff officers in the German Army. Heinemann was at Wachtel's elbow. In face of the facts, he cannot have needed much convincing that there was no chance of a successful salvo in a quarter of an hour's time. Having talked the corps commander over, a British officer in Wachtel's position would hardly, one might suppose, have bothered much about corps headquarters beyond telling someone to get them on the telephone and put them in the picture. Yet Wachtel, with much to do and only a few minutes left in which to do it, took the trouble to put through a call to Walter at Maisons-Lafitte and ask him to sanction the postponement. Walter refused. Heinemann then took the telephone from Wachtel, and had to assert his authority over his own Chief of Staff before the programme could be changed.

As Wachtel might have foreseen and perhaps did foresee, an hour was not nearly enough to put matters right. In the light of further reports he ordered at 11.50 p.m. that no salvo should be attempted before half-past three, but that sites should begin 'harassing fire' as they became ready.

Soon afterwards the long-range guns near Cap Gris Nez opened fire on towns in Kent, as they had done on many occasions since the summer of 1940. Nearly four hundred civilians living near the Straits of Dover had been killed or seriously injured by cross-Channel shelling since the beginning of the war. But a new departure was that, for the first time, at least one place well away from the coast was included in the target-list. Between midnight and four o'clock twenty-four rounds fell at Folkestone, which was not unusual, but in addition eight hit Maidstone, while one round, probably intended for the same target, landed at the village of Otham, two-and-a-half miles to the south-east. It is tempting to assume that Heinemann or Wachtel arranged the bombardment as a stop-gap, but there is no proof that they did, or that they were in a position to ask the gunners to help them out. An air raid on London, which was to have coincided with Wachtel's salvo, had been cancelled on the ground that all bombers were needed for attacks on the bridgehead in Normandy, and the most probable explanation of the shelling is that it was meant to hinder the assembly of reserve divisions which were being held in Kent as part of the Allied deception-plan.

As things turned out, there was no salvo, either at half-past three or later. In the outcome only ten missiles were despatched by long-suffering launching-teams before even 'harassing fire' was called off. Five crashed almost at once, a sixth disappeared into the unknown and probably came down in the Channel, and the remaining four reached England. The first to arrive was the author of the 'swishing sound' and vintage-model noises which betrayed its identity to the Royal Observer Corps before it fell at Swanscombe; the three which followed came to earth at Cuckfield, in Sussex, Bethnal Green, in the East End of London, and Platt, near Sevenoaks in Kent. There were no casualties except at Bethnal Green, where a railway bridge was demolished and where six people were killed and nine injured. In the absence of Heinemann, presumably still on his way back from Wachtel's command post or sleeping after his long vigil there, Walter soon afterwards ordered on his behalf that no more launchings should be attempted until the causes of the night's fiasco became clear, and that all sites should be camouflaged. He then threatened Wachtel with a court martial, which Wachtel said afterwards he would have welcomed, since it would have established that he had done everything a commander could do without the right tools for the job.

How much sleep the regimental commander succeeded in getting between the time of his return from Maisons-Lafitte on June 11 and the morning of June 16 is not recorded. At any rate he and his subordinates did not waste much time. By dusk on June 15 the shortcomings of the night of June 12 and the early hours of June 13 had been investigated, and the threat of disciplinary action had been beaten off. All sites where launching-rails had been installed were adequately supplied with fuel, missiles and equipment, and the regiment was in good heart for a true beginning after its earlier and disastrous attempt to beat the clock.

6

Engagement : Phase One

JUST after four o'clock in the morning on June 13, 1944, the member of the Royal Observer Corps who afterwards described the first flying bomb to reach this country as passing his post in Kent with a 'swishing sound' alerted the defences by shouting into his telephone the code-word 'Diver'. A few minutes later the message reached the operations-room at Stanmore where, between three and four years earlier, the watch-keeping staff of Fighter Command had studied, for eight months on end, the nightly build-up of the 'Blitz' on a squared map as large as a fair-sized room.

Leigh-Mallory's emotions when he awoke to the news that attacks with pilotless aircraft had begun are not hard to guess. A deeply-felt dismay that the expenditure of twenty-three thousand tons of bombs on the ski sites had not, after all, prevented the Germans from using their new weapon, perhaps also a gnawing suspicion that the threat from the 'modified' sites had been too lightly brushed aside, were doubtless tempered by the reflection that the attack might not amount to very much and that Hill and his subordinates could be trusted to deal competently with it so far as purely defensive counter-measures went. The fact remained that a storm long expected had broken at the very moment when the skies seemed to men who shared Leigh-Mallory's high-level viewpoint to be clearing.

To Hill, on the other hand, it must have been obvious from the start that the new development, no matter how regrettable from the humanitarian point of view, might give him the chance of proving his abilities which every normally ambitious commander welcomes. He soon saw, however, that Wachtel's opening effort was far too small to justify the special deployment called for in his 'Diver' plan. At their usual morning meeting the Chiefs of Staff endorsed his decision to see what the next few days might bring before ordering balloons and guns to move. Meanwhile anti-aircraft gunners and fighter-pilots would be free to engage Wachtel's missiles, if any came, on the same terms as ordinary aircraft.

The Chiefs of Staff then went on to discuss offensive countermeasures. Hill had already arranged that a number of the 'intruder' aircraft whose normal job was to harass German bomber-bases should make a visual reconnaissance of those of the 'modified' sites which seemed most likely to have been used during the past few hours. His assumption that some, at least, of the missiles launched during the night had come from the 'modified' sites could not be seriously questioned in the light of the air photographs taken on June 11, although it still seemed possible that ski sites were in use as well. The great question was whether a substantial part of the Allied bomber effort should be switched from the battle in Normandy or the bombing of Germany to the rather daunting task of knocking out all known 'modified' sites and possibly a few ski sites for good measure.

The Chief of the Air Staff, Air Chief Marshal Portal, was reluctant to switch bombers to the 'modified' sites. Calculating that many thousands of sorties would be needed to knock them out but that a thousand should suffice to deal with four of the eight structures which Allied intelligence officers called supply sites, he concluded that bombing the latter rather than the former would prove the better bargain. This was admirable reasoning apart from one not inconsiderable flaw: there was no proof that Wachtel was using the supply sites, and some evidence to suggest that he was not. Air Chief Marshal Portal could not know that the Germans had given up the idea of using the supply sites about the time when they abandoned the ski sites, for no one on his side of the Channel knew it. But he must have been very badly briefed indeed if he did not know that the intelligence staffs had never found any firm link to connect the supply sites with the ski sites, although the connection did exist; that no link at all had been found to connect them with the 'modified' sites; and that trial attacks on one supply site to test the enemy's response had yielded negative results. Unless the Germans were acting out of character by bluffing, a fair inference was that that particular supply site, at any rate, had ceased to hold much interest for them. Nor had the Allies received any indication, during the whole of the long period when a great part of their attention was focused on the area where the supply sites lay, that the enemy was moving supplies to the sites either to support a secret-weapons offensive or for any other purpose.

Lord Cherwell, who was present in his capacity as Scientific Adviser to the Prime Minister and Minister of Defence, had the reputation in some circles of distrusting most proposals not inspired by himself. For once, at any rate, he exercised his scepticism on the side of commonsense when he pointed to the danger of merely *assuming* that the supply sites were important. Nevertheless the prospect of giving Wachtel's organisation a hard knock at the cost of only a thousand sorties was so attractive that Cherwell's warning was disregarded. Later in the day the War Cabinet agreed that the Supreme Commander should be asked to sanction 'heavy attacks' on the supply sites. The 'modified' sites were also commended to his attention, but in terms which gave him a ready-made pretext to put them on a low order of priority.

The result was that the new phase of offensive counter-measures got off to a poor start. Between June 13 and June 15 heavy bombers of the United States Eighth Air Force made repeated attacks on valueless supply sites, but no action was taken against 'modified' sites apart from the reconnaissance arranged by Hill.

About 10 p.m. on June 15 Wachtel redeemed his earlier failure by making a new beginning with adequate equipment and a certain amount of dearly-bought experience. During the next fourteen hours his troops launched 244 missiles from sites aligned on London, in addition to fifty or so aimed at South-ampton or places near it. Forty-five of the missiles intended for London crashed almost immediately, but a fair proportion of the rest reached the huge target presented by the London Civil Defence Region. British reports showed later that 144 of 155 missiles observed by the defences up to midnight on June 16 crossed the coast and that just over half of them came down in Greater London. Wides or overshoots included one as far afield as Norfolk, but undershoots were much more common. More than two-thirds of the missiles which did reach London fell south of the Thames. The defences brought down thirty-three missiles, not always with the effect intended. In accordance with the sanction given on June 13, the gunners of the London Inner Artillery Zone opened fire enthusiastically, believing that missiles hit would explode more or less harmlessly in the air. As things turned out, eleven of those brought down fell in London's built-up area, among them some which might conceivably have come down in open country if they had been left to complete their course.

On the morning of June 16 Hill had no difficulty in concluding that the time had come to order the 'Diver' deployment, and once more the Chiefs of Staff agreed with him. Partly in consequence of the authority which he and General Pile had been granted early in the year to take preliminary steps on the assumption that their first and more ambitious plan might have to be put into effect, the moves were completed in little more than a third of the time allowed in their revised plan. Air Vice-Marshal Gell, of Balloon Command, brought off an astonishing feat by shifting five hundred barrage-balloons to new sites on the Cobham-Limpsfield ridge in about five days. General Pile, with even more awkward problems to solve, was so little behind him that nearly all the guns, as well as all the balloons, were ready for action in their new positions by June 21.

Soon after the order to deploy went out on June 16, the Home Secretary and Minister of Home Security, Mr Herbert Morrison, told the House of Commons that the country was under bombardment with pilotless aircraft, soon more widely known as flying bombs. The news struck many members of the public as eerie, the sequel as even more frightening than the orthodox air attacks with which Londoners had become familiar. There was something peculiarly menacing about the death-rattle of an Argus duct approaching the end of its short useful life, something more sinister still about the brief hush which followed the interruption of the fuel-supply as the missile swung into a dive which ended with a shattering explosion as the nose hit the ground or collided with a building.* Over the whole period of the offensive, the number of people killed by flying bombs was less than one for every missile which crossed the coast or came within range of the defences; but the area of superficial damage was so wide, the whole business so alarming, that the orderly retreat to the relatively peaceful

---

* The missile dived, at the same time altering its course slightly, under the influence of a device which took effect when a small windmill in the nose had made a predetermined number of revolutions. The cut-out of the propulsion-unit as the missile took up the diving position, which did not always occur but was often noticed, seems to have been more or less unforeseen, the probability being that the general expectation when the weapon was first tested was that it would make a power-dive.

countryside of a hundred thousand Londoners a week for ten weeks on end was not at all surprising.

Later on that same first day after Wachtel's successful resumption of the offensive the Prime Minister, presumably acting in his capacity as Minister of Defence although no precise definition seems to have been attempted of the roles which he and others present were supposed to be playing on this particular occasion, held what was rather bafflingly called a 'staff conference' attended by the Chiefs of Staff or their representatives, the Secretary of State for Air and the Deputy Supreme Commander. Hill and Pile were also present. Thereupon Hill was authorised, in terms which afterwards became of some importance, to 'redistribute the gun, searchlight and balloon defences, as necessary, to counter the attacks', with the proviso that he should act in consultation with Pile, as he would have done in any case. This time not exposed to sardonic reminders from Cherwell that assumption was not evidence, the strategists went on to agree that the Supreme Commander should be asked to take all possible measures to 'neutralise' the supply and launching sites, 'subject to no interference with the essential requirements of the battle in France'. This decision may have looked good in the minutes, yet any intelligence officer acquainted with the subject would have known that by 'supply sites' the Chiefs of Staff meant not sites which Wachtel was known to be using for supply, but sites which he was not known to be using.

Meanwhile Leigh-Mallory, too, was busy. He had been made responsible for co-ordinating offensive counter-measures to long-range weapons when attacks on the ski sites began in the previous December; at least nominally, he still remained so. In the course of the day he satisfied himself that, according to the Air Ministry, the best targets were four supply sites, followed on a lower order of priority by eleven ski sites and on a still lower one by twelve 'modified' sites. The astonishing thing about this target list was not that the Germans had, in fact, abandoned both the supply sites and the ski sites, for the Air Ministry had no proof of that. The facts which threw a damning light on the source of Leigh-Mallory's information were that there was not, and never had been, any evidence that the supply sites were in use; that one of the reasons, if not the only reason, for including ski sites at all was that no 'modified' sites had yet been discovered in an area from which some flying bombs appeared to have come; and that, on the other hand, the 'modified' sites which ranked below them all showed signs of recent use.

Armed with the paradoxical conclusion that twelve 'modified' sites from which flying bombs had almost certainly been launched within the last few days were less worthy of attack than eleven ski sites whose value to the enemy was purely conjectural, and that the best targets of all were four supply sites whose place in the system had never been established, Leigh-Mallory asked Air Chief Marshal Harris of Bomber Command to follow up the American effort against the supply sites by bombing them as soon as possible. Harris did so, sending substantial forces to all four sites on the next two nights. Thus, by the morning of June 18 all four had been heavily bombed in the course of the past four or five days, at least two of them in daylight by the Americans as well as in darkness by the British.

At that point Harris dug his toes in. He was not, he said, prepared to devote any further effort to the supply sites without proof that it was needed. This was not mere obstinacy but good sense. By June 18 there was evidence that the Germans had installations of some importance at Nucourt, Saint-Leu-d'Esserent and Rilly-la-Montagne. There was also evidence that they had three depots which seemed to play an important part in the secret-weapons programme. As yet there was no cast-iron link between these two sets of facts and inferences, but the case for believing that Nucourt, Saint-Leu-d'Esserent and Rilly-la-Montagne might be the missing flying bomb stores was at least as good as the case for believing that further bombing of the supply sites could show a dividend. At the same time, neither Harris nor his American counterpart, General Doolittle, was satisfied with the place allotted in the Air Ministry's target-list to the 'modified' sites. By June 18 nearly seventy such sites had been discovered. The two commanders felt sure that they would never be knocked out by spasmodic attacks delivered at odd moments when sorties could be spared for targets of low priority. If they were to be tackled at all, the proper way was to deal them a crushing blow, on the highest priority, at the right moment.

As it happened, June 18 was a Sunday. At twenty minutes past eleven that morning a flying bomb hit the Royal Military Chapel at Wellington Barracks, barely a quarter of a mile from Buckingham Palace and not much further from the government offices sandwiched between Whitehall and St James's Park. Seventy-eight civilians and a hundred and eleven members of the fighting services attending morning service were killed or seriously injured. No flying bomb up to that moment had inflicted anything like as many casualties; none had just missed killing so many people who survived to recount their experiences in governmental and official circles and in clubs frequented by men close to the seat of power. Just as even the most humanitarian of men is more profoundly impressed by a calamity on his own doorstep than by a typhoon which sweeps away a dozen villages on the far side of the world, so that morning's disaster brought home the menace of Hitler's new weapon as no dispassionate scrutiny of casualty returns could ever do.

On the same day General Eisenhower ruled that, until further notice, attacks on long-range weapon targets must take precedence over everything except the urgent requirements of the battle across the Channel. Two days later the War

Cabinet gave Mr Sandys a watching brief over counter-measures to long-range weapons as chairman of a new 'Crossbow' Committee. Neither of these events prevented Air Chief Marshal Portal from grudging any large-scale diversion from attacks on the German oil industry, described by Air Chief Marshal Harris as a 'panacea target'.* Nor did they end the reluctance of Harris and Doolittle to plug away at targets of such doubtful value as supply sites and 'large sites'. But a big step forward was taken a day or two later when Nucourt and Saint-Leu-d'Esserent were firmly identified as V.1 stores, and were added to the Air Ministry's hitherto defective and still imperfect target-list.

During the last week in June the United States Eighth Air Force made heavy attacks on both Nucourt and Saint-Leu-d'Esserent. The British Bomber Command attacked Saint-Leu on the night of July 4 and again three nights later. These attacks were followed by a significant drop in the number of missiles approaching the United Kingdom, which fell for ten days after July 7 from an average of a hundred a day to fewer than seventy. But the big step forward was not followed up. Nucourt was bombed on three more occasions before the middle of July, and sixty-eight 'modified' sites were tackled by that date, it now seems without much success. But the Allied effort continued during the rest of the campaign to be spread over a wide range of objectives, some of them believed at the time to be of doubtful relevance, and some now known to have been of no relevance at all. Thus the real job of countering the V.1 offensive was left to the air defences, with some assistance after the middle of August from the Allied armies sweeping on towards the launching-area.

---

* Harris, *op. cit.*, p. 220. Harris wrote after the war that the offensive against oil was a complete success, but one which could not reasonably be expected when the attacks were undertaken. The Allied strategists 'bet on an outsider, and it happened to win the race'.

II

From the start of the V.1 offensive two points were clear to Hill. The first was that a few hundred guns whose number was never thought more than barely adequate to meet the scale of attack expected from the few ski sites assumed to have escaped destruction would not suffice to meet the larger one of which the 'modified' sites were capable. The second was that one of his biggest problems would be to prevent the various arms of the defence from getting in each other's way. In the outline plan which he drew up in December, he had stressed that fighters, guns, searchlights and balloons would have to be used 'in such a manner as to avoid causing mutual interference'.

To meet the first point, he soon arranged for the deployment of many more than the 192 heavy and 192 light guns contemplated for the period after D-day in his truncated February plan. By June 28, 363 and 422 light guns of Anti-Aircraft Command were in action, and further weapons, among them rocket-projectors, light guns manned by the Royal Air Force Regiment and anti-aircraft vehicles of the Royal Armoured Corps, were either in position or on the way. He also arranged to double the strength of the balloon barrage in Kent and Surrey by drawing on all other barrages throughout the country except that at Scapa Flow, and then to add another 750 balloons within a week. The number of balloons thus rose to 1,000 by the beginning of July and to 1,750 by July 8.

To deal with the second point was very much harder. Between December and February, when Hill and Pile were working on their successive plans for deployment of the guns, jamming by the enemy of the gunners' radar sets was so much feared that, wherever possible, 'dead ground' sites in folds and hollows of the North Downs were chosen at the cost of exposing the sets to a certain amount of interference from natural features. Allied bombing of German installations immediately before D-day was so successful that jamming ceased to be much of a danger by the time the February plan was put into effect; but to change the whole scheme at the last moment, even if anyone had thought of doing it, would have meant throwing away all the benefits of the preliminary measures which made it possible to complete the deployment quickly. The result was that the heavy and light guns earmarked moved soon after the middle of June to their allotted positions on the North Downs, where they were soon joined by reinforcements, but that a growing number of light guns which there was no special reason to confine to the Downs were sited during the next few weeks in positions which gave them the best chance of engaging Wachtel's missiles as they crossed the coast. By the middle of July nearly eight hundred guns of various calibres were deployed on the chalk hills of Kent and Surrey, but there were also about six hundred light guns which were not in the gun-belt at all but many miles to the south of it.

The tendency of light guns to proliferate outside the gun-belt added to difficulties always present where weapons belonging to different services are used on the same battleground, but the problem was bound to arise in any case. Right at the beginning of Wachtel's offensive Hill gave guns and fighters each a separate sphere of action by forbidding pilots to fly over the gun-belt. After a few days, however, he came to the conclusion that this meant getting less than the full benefit from his fighters, especially when the weather favoured them. The solution he adopted from June 19 until the middle of July, therefore, was to give the fighters complete freedom of action when the weather was particularly good, and in such circumstances the guns were not allowed to fire. Conversely, in bad weather the fighters were grounded and the gunners had complete freedom. When the weather was neither one thing nor the other, fighters were excluded from the gun-belt and the gunners were allowed to fire up to 8,000 feet, with the proviso that a pilot in actual pursuit of a missile might enter the gun-belt and was then entitled to expect that fire would be withheld. Broadly the same rules applied to gunners outside the belt, except that they were not allowed to fire at all in middling weather unless they were linked to Anti-Aircraft Command's communications network and were quite sure that they could see their targets and that no fighters were about.

Himself an active pilot who flew many sorties against flying bombs, Hill had no difficulty in understanding why his subordinates did not always stick to these rules and were sometimes fired at even when they did. Dealing with flying bombs, he said, was like joining in a very fast game of rugger played on a very small ground. Even his fastest aircraft had such a small margin of superiority over the V.1 in point of speed that he found it expedient to modify some of them, even to the extent of stripping off their paint and polishing their external surfaces, to make them just a little faster. The missiles, crossing the coast at roughly 340 miles an hour and reaching their top speed of roughly 400 miles an hour as they approached London, covered the thirty miles to the southern edge of the gun-belt in five minutes. The chances that a pilot skimming at six miles a minute through indifferent weather would inadvertently enter the belt even when he was not technically in pursuit of a missile were so high that only extreme vigilance and self-restraint on the part of the gunners could ever have made the system work.

The essential problem for a pilot aiming to bring down a flying bomb before it reached the gun-belt, or at any rate short of the balloon-barrage, was not, however, to find enough speed to catch the quarry after a stern chase for which there was seldom room, but to put himself in the right position to intercept. If he was flying high, and the terrestrial background was not too confusing, he might hope to see a missile to landward of him and catch it up by diving on it; but more often success depended on his spotting one which had not passed him. Shell-bursts, signal-rockets and a running commentary from radar stations or Royal Observer Corps Centres could all help him, but much of the help had to come from his own eyesight. Once he had picked out his target, the problem of bringing it down was all his, unless another pilot happened to have chosen the same missile and forestalled him. Different pilots had different ideas as to how the business should be done, but generally the approved method was for the attacker to put himself on the same course as the target, allow it to draw up with him, and fire obliquely at it from a safe distance of not less than two hundred yards as it went by. The temptation to come to closer grips with a target which could not fire back was strong, but at least five pilots were killed in the course of Wachtel's offensive because they gave way to it and had their machines wrecked by the explosion of missiles at too short a range. Perhaps for that reason, or perhaps merely because they liked unorthodox methods or did not trust their shooting, some pilots preferred not to use their guns at all, but to get so close to a missile that they could tip it over by putting a wing under it and then banking sharply, or capsize it simply by letting their slipstream play on it. A few missiles are said to have been made by similar treatment to turn on to new courses which took them out to sea.

Largely because there was so little elbow-room between the coast and the North Downs, alleged infractions of the rule that pilots must not enter the gun-belt in indifferent weather unless actually in pursuit of a missile were so numerous during the first few weeks of the offensive that Hill soon had cause to question the soundness of the concession he had made. He found, too, that even pilots strongly suspected of breaking the rule were invariably aggrieved when they were shot at, not always understanding how hard it was for gunners themselves engaging one of a number of missiles which might be in the air at once to see that a fighter had entered their field of fire. On his frequent visits to fighter bases, he was shown many aircraft whose condition proved beyond question that they had been fired at by the guns.

At the same time, it was obvious that all was not well with the gunners. Wachtel's missiles, each one flying on a steady course and, for all practical purposes, at a constant height and speed, might have been expected to make perfect targets for anti-aircraft gunnery, yet for some weeks results were extremely disappointing. Between the opening of the offensive and the middle of July the guns brought down only 261 flying bombs, in addition to one shared with other arms, as compared with 924 brought down by fighters and 55 by balloons. This was partly, but only partly, because the bombs flew, as Hill had feared they would, at just the height which the gunners found most awkward. At 2,000 to 3,000 feet they were too high to give the light guns the best chance of success, yet crossed the field of vision of the gunners at the 'heavy' sites so rapidly that crews barely had time to use their radar and predictors and lay their guns before the target was out of range. Permanently emplaced guns which were electrically elevated and traversed had a big advantage over mobile guns in that respect, but to use them seemed scarcely feasible until Pile's staff of Royal Electrical and Mechanical Engineers, under Brigadier J. A. E. Burls, produced a portable platform, popularly called the 'Pile Mattress', which saved weeks of work and vast quantities of concrete. About the end of June, Pile also improved the chances of the heavy guns by moving many of them to higher ground where their radar sets worked better, at the same time concentrating in front of them the light guns previously at searchlight sites.

But the difficulties which prevented the guns from making their full contribution were not merely technical. They were also psychological. The gunners faced the knowledge that, no matter how much their equipment might improve, no matter how perfect their organisation might become, a great many targets which they would have liked to engage were bound to pass them unscathed as long as the rules for engagement which Hill had adopted on June 19 and codified a week later were in force. That they had to remain idle for the benefit of the fighters on days of perfect visibility, when even their training was restricted, was bad enough; the rule which called upon them to hold their fire whenever a pilot chose to chase a missile into the gun-belt in indifferent weather was still more irksome. If pilots could complain that gunners broke the rule by continuing to shoot when they ought to have stopped shooting, so could gunners argue that pilots abused it by entering the gun-belt without good reason. Moreover, these intrusions seemed to the gunners always to occur just when they were engaging a target which they were sure they could have brought down if they had not been interrupted.

The performance of the defences as a whole showed a fairly steady upward trend during the first five weeks of the offensive, the proportion of missiles destroyed to missiles observed rising from about a fifth immediately before the deployment and rather less than two-fifths immediately after it to more than two-fifths at the beginning of July and well over half during the period of reduced activity which followed the bombing of Saint-Leu-d'Esserent. But this improvement brought Hill only qualified satisfaction, even though it played the chief part in reducing the number of missiles reaching London from more than seventy a day to roughly forty and finally to twenty-five. Observing that the fighters were doing well but the gunners badly, he saw that partial victory over the flying bomb would be too dearly bought if the effect was to leave half his team suffering from a sense of frustration which was bound to lessen their efficiency.

On July 10 he made up his mind to cut the Gordian knot. Concluding that he could not afford a temporary success at the cost of impairing, perhaps for ever, the spirit of co-operation between guns and fighters which he and his prede-cessors had built up since the beginning of the war, he decided to take the heroic step of excluding fighters from the gun-belt in all circumstances after the middle of the month. Only a bold man could have made that decision, and only a commander who had proved that his heart was with his pilots could hope to carry it through without making himself desperately un-popular in squadrons.

At a conference summoned to discuss the change, General Pile suggested that a logical corollary was to move into the gun-belt all guns at present outside it, with the exception of a few which might be left on the coast to pinpoint incoming missiles by firing marker-bursts. Guns and fighters would then have clearly distinguishable fields of action, and all gunners except the inconsiderable minority still outside the gun-belt would be free to train in all weathers without fear of breaking rules or harming fighters.

These arguments struck Hill with great force. There was also the point that removal of all guns into the gun-belt would go some way to compensate pilots for their exclusion from it by giving them a clear run from the Channel to the North Downs. Before the conference broke up, he asked for detailed proposals and promised to consider them, the implication being that he would accept them unless they disclosed some unexpec-ted snag. He then told his Deputy Senior Air Staff Officer, Air Commodore G. H. Ambler, to draw up a paper explaining to pilots why they were to be banished from the gun-belt.

7

Engagement : Phase Two

AIR Commodore Ambler was not a professional airman but a Yorkshire textile merchant who looked forward to resuming his old place in a flourishing family concern when the war was over. As with all staff officers, his value depended largely on his ability to clear his mind of preconceptions, and he had the advantage over many of not being so steeped in service tradition that he needed to make any special effort to convince himself that senior officers could be wrong. He did not quarrel with his chief's decision to exclude fighters from the gun-belt, or dissent from Pile's argument that all the guns ought to be in one place. Yet the more he thought about these things, the more strongly did he feel that there was a fallacy in the conclusion that the guns on the coast must be moved to the North Downs.

To test his reasoning, he decided to commit his thoughts to paper 'strictly in accordance with the recommended method contained in the War Manual'. The result came out just the same. Hill's object was not simply to redress a grievance, but to put the gunners in the best position to exploit their ability to shoot down targets which could not dodge. That position was surely the coast, where they would have an unrestricted field of fire over the widest possible arc, where their radar sets would suffer the least interference from neighbouring contours, and where, incidentally, any rounds that failed to explode would fall harmlessly in the sea. The last point was important since fuses which automatically exploded anti-aircraft shells in the vicinity of the target were coming into service. Shells so fused were supposed to blow themselves up before they reached the ground if they failed to get near enough to the target for the proximity-fuse to work, but the self-destroying device was not yet so reliable that the new system of fusing could safely be used where unexploded rounds might fall on houses. On the coast the gunners would be free to fire proximity-fused shells with a clear conscience.

Ambler finished his paper during the night of July 12. Next morning Sir Robert Watson Watt, the inventor of radar and a telecommunications expert, happened to call at Hill's headquarters. He confirmed that the gunners' radar sets would work best near the sea, and told Ambler that he, too, had formed the opinion that the South Coast was the right place for the gunbelt. To move it there would mean splitting the field of action of the fighters in two, but that seemed to Ambler a disadvantage which would be more than outweighed by the advantage of a much better deal for the guns. To some extent interception over the land and interception over the sea were, in any case, separate problems. Pilots over the sea relied largely on the radar early-warning system to put them on to their targets, while pilots over the land depended more on the Royal Observer Corps and on such pointers as shell-bursts, signal rockets and searchlight beams.

Impressed by Ambler's arguments and Watson Watt's endorsement of them, Hill decided to give himself the better part of the day to think things over and make sure that no technical flaw had been overlooked. He asked General Pile to brief himself for a conference in the late afternoon, prevailed on Watson Watt to attend also, and summoned Air Vice-Marshal Saunders, commanding No. 11 Group, from his headquarters at Uxbridge. In addition he arranged that Leigh-Mallory should be represented.

Pile came to the conference prepared to give a warm welcome to Ambler's proposal, but with no intention of showing excessive zeal. Placing the gun-belt on the coast had been considered earlier at his headquarters, but such a radical change had seemed so unlikely to be accepted by airmen that the idea was not pursued. From his point of view it was clearly better that support should come from the air force.

Such support was, in fact, forthcoming, not only from Hill's staff but also from Air Vice-Marshal Saunders. Far from objecting that the field of action of his fighters would be cut in two, as he might have been expected to do, Saunders described Ambler's plan as certainly the best that had yet been produced.

Before the end of the meeting, Hill made up his mind that the gun-belt must be moved. The question he had then to decide was whether to order the move at once, or refer the matter to higher authority with a strong recommendation in favour of the change, and then sit back and await the outcome. Either course could be justified, the first on the ground that he had been authorised on June 16 to redistribute the defences as necessary and that this was no more than a necessary redistribution; the second on the ground that he would not have moved guns from Manchester to the gun-belt without formal sanction from above, and that re-siting the gun-belt was a far more momentous step than merely moving guns from Manchester.

It did not take him long to conclude that he must act at once. Literally and metaphorically, Pile's batteries were digging in on the North Downs, where already thirty-two of the static guns which were being substituted for mobile pieces had been emplaced. As yet it was not too late to uproot the gun-belt, but soon it might be. If Hill referred the question to the Air Staff, and if they referred it to the Chiefs of Staff or to the committee which usually considered proposals to move guns from one defended area to another, several days might elapse before a decision could be taken. On every one of them the case for leaving the guns where they were would grow stronger. It was now or never.

When Pile left the conference to return to his headquarters a few hundred yards away, he took with him Hill's authority, as air defence commander, to order his batteries to redeploy. Within a few hours arrangements were in train to shift 23,000 men and women, with about eight hundred guns and some 60,000 tons of stores and ammunition, from the North Downs to the coast, and to re-lay about 3,000 miles of cable. By July 17 all the heavy guns were in their new positions. At sunrise on July 19 nearly sixteen hundred guns of various calibres, in addition to some two hundred rocket-projectors, were ready for action along the seventy-mile stretch of coast from St Margaret's Bay to Cuckmere Haven.

Immediately after the conference Hill told Leigh-Mallory what he had done. Leigh-Mallory asked whether a trial deployment on a short stretch of coast would not have been better, but made no further comment when Hill answered that it was all or nothing and that half-measures were worse than useless.

The Air Staff at the Air Ministry were not so easily silenced. Believing that Hill had sacrificed the fighter force for the benefit of the guns, and suspecting that he had yielded to pressure from General Pile and perhaps from Mr Sandys as Chairman of the War Cabinet 'Crossbow' Committee and a former gunner-officer in the Territorial Army, they took him to task for ordering the move without consulting them. He ought, they said, at least to have given them a chance of sending a representative to his conference on July 13.

Whether they were right on a strict interpretation of the protocol governing these matters is a nice point. Irrespective of the precise significance of the authority given to Hill on June 16 to redistribute the defences, Hill was answerable in the

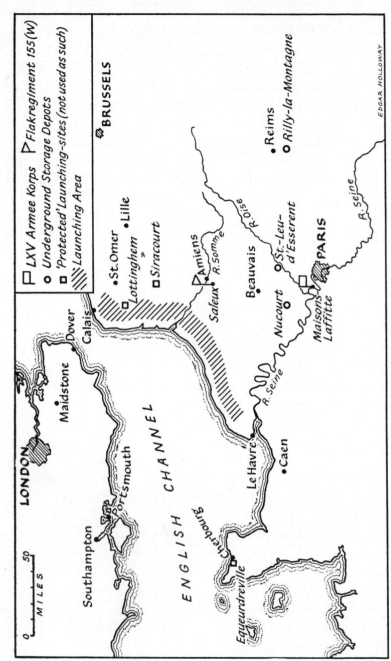

Legend:
- ⊓ LXV Armee Korps
- ⊓ Flakregiment 155(W)
- ○ Underground Storage Depots
- ◻ 'Protected' Launching-sites (not used as such)
- ▨ Launching Area

LONDON

Maidstone
Dover
Calais

Southampton
Portsmouth

Cherbourg
Equeurdreville ◻

E N G L I S H   C H A N N E L

Le Havre ●
● Caen

Dover
Calais
St.Omer ●
Lottingham ○
◻ Siracourt
●Lille

△ Amiens
Saleux ●
R. Somme
R. Oise
Beauvais ●
Nucourt ○
St.-Leu- ○
d'Esserent
Maisons- ◻
Laffitte
PARIS
R. Seine
R. Seine

⊞ BRUSSELS

● Reims
○ Rilly-la-Montagne

R. Seine

MILES
0 _____ 50

EDGAR HOLLOWAY

V.I ORGANISATION: SUMMER 1944

first place to Leigh-Mallory for his exercise of the powers delegated to him when the Allied Expeditionary Air Force was set up. Leigh-Mallory *was* represented at Hill's conference, and he tacitly condoned Hill's decision, even if he did not expressly sanction it, at a time when the move could still have been countermanded. It could be argued that the Air Staff's remonstrance ought to have been addressed to Leigh-Mallory rather than to Hill. On the other hand, Leigh-Mallory would not himself have interpreted the position so strictly as to raise any objection if Hill had asked the Air Staff to send a representative to his conference, and there is no doubt that Hill knowingly staked his professional reputation on the success of the move rather than court delay by consulting them. What he did not expect was that they would be quite so prompt to remind him of what he already knew.

He soon found, however, that he had bought himself a new freedom. The Air Staff might not relish being by-passed, but no one could fail to respect a commander who had the courage of his convictions and was willing to risk his career to get things done. Once it was apparent that no outside pressure had been brought to bear on him, nothing more was needed to consolidate his standing than that the experiment should succeed.

At first, he was not sure that it would. Officially, the new system went into force at dawn on July 17. During the next six days 204 flying bombs reached London out of 473 which approached the country. The defences made a creditable showing, especially between sunset on July 20 and sunset on July 21, when guns and fighters between them brought down forty-three missiles and the balloons another seventeen; but their performance was not quite as good as in the last week under the old system, and that of the fighters was noticeably worse.

On reflection, Hill decided that these results were not too bad. At any rate he had no cause to feel disheartened. The gunners were already doing better than before the move, although they had barely had time to get used to their new positions; that the number of missiles brought down by fighters should show at least a temporary falling-off was no more than he had expected. A commander more easily satisfied than Hill might have concluded that all was well and that ruffled feelings at the Air Ministry would soon cease to matter if overall results in the next few weeks showed an upward trend.

Characteristically, he did not draw that conclusion. He had given the gunners their new deal, and they were making good use of their opportunities. His job now, as he saw it, was to encourage his squadrons to work harder than ever in order to ensure that they took their fair toll of missiles over the Channel and allowed no missile which got through the gun-belt to reach London if it was humanly possible for them to bring it down. The balloon barrage, already made as dense as was practically feasible and extended slightly to the west to cover a wider arc, was the last line of defence. Perfection would be attained only when gunners and fighter-pilots allowed no bomb to reach it.

Again characteristically, the method he chose was personal contact with stations and squadrons. A pilot himself, he knew that operational instructions and tactical memoranda were no substitute for the spoken word. There were able men on the staff at Stanmore, but they had their jobs to do, and they could not move as fast as he did. Saunders and his staff at Uxbridge were preoccupied with innumerable tasks arising from the battle in Normandy: Sector Headquarters at Biggin Hill had become a centre for the hour-to-hour co-ordination of defensive counter-measures, but the Sector Commander and his staff had neither the time nor the authority to act as evangelists of tactical and moral doctrine. So the work for which subordinates could not be spared was done by the Air Marshal Commanding. Leaving his office a little before half-past twelve,

Hill could be airborne in his Spitfire over Northolt less than twenty minutes later, and in the Officers' Mess of a station on the edge of the new gun-belt by one o'clock. Pilots for whom most visits from highly-placed officers were an ordeal, and who never saw Leigh-Mallory, found in the air defence commander a fellow-craftsman who spoke their language with authority, and whose views on the art of joining the hunt for flying bombs were worth hearing, since he had joined it yesterday and would be joining it again to-morrow.

At some stations, Hill was shown fragments of shell-casing which had fallen on aerodromes or penetrated aircraft. From the middle of July his standard reply when pilots alleged that such exhibits proved the incompetence or irresponsibility of Pile's gunners was that the move to the coast had brought battery headquarters conveniently close to air force stations, and that the complainant or his commanding officer could not do better than go and discuss his grievances with his opposite number in the other service. Calls exchanged at his suggestion between army and air force officers gave some of his subordinates their first glimpse of the possibility that anti-aircraft gunners as well as airmen might have their difficulties. No longer content to blame the soldiers for all mistakes, station and squadron commanders became noticeably readier to jump on pilots who jeopardised their aircraft by breaking rules and flouting commonsense.

About the end of July the overall performance of the defences began to improve considerably. The proportion of missiles destroyed to missiles observed, after falling off in the first week after redeployment, climbed steadily to 74 per cent. in the third week in August, fell back in the next week to 62 per cent., then rose again to 83 per cent. Over the whole of the seven-week period from the middle of July to early September, the figure was nearly 60 per cent. as compared with roughly 40 per cent. during the first five weeks of the offensive.

Observing that the effectiveness of the guns increased more than three-fold during those seven weeks as compared with their achievement during the earlier period, while that of the fighters declined by only a third in spite of their exclusion from the new gun-belt and the barrier thrown across their field of action, Hill concluded that his proven ability to get more out of the guns without getting correspondingly less out of the fighters was largely due to better team-work. Even if the figures did not go the whole way to prove his case, at any rate they were striking vindication of his decision to move the guns. With the guns destroying 170 bombs a week after the change as compared with 50 a week before it, and the fighters 120 a week as compared with 180, not even his sternest critic could claim that he had made anything but a good bargain.

The move to the coast was certainly the chief cause of the vast improvement in the performance of the guns after the middle of July, but it was not the only cause. Other factors were the addition to the gun-belt by mid-August of another 180 heavy and 38 light guns and some hundreds of rocket-projectors, chiefly from British but partly from American sources; the continued substitution of static for mobile guns; and, more important still, the increasing adoption of new radar sets and predictors made in the United States but reflecting British ideas of what was needed. The fighters gained some benefit from the introduction of the jet-propelled Meteor about the middle of August, but the aircraft used for most sorties were the Tempest V, the Spitfire XIV, the Mustang III, and at night the Mosquito. The Mustangs were borrowed by Hill from Air Marshal Coningham of the Second Tactical Air Force, who lent him at first a squadron and later a whole wing.

Within a fortnight of Hill's fateful decision of July 13, any fear that the redeployment might prove a blunder thus disappeared. By the middle of August Hill was confident that he could bring down between one-half and three-quarters of all targets, irrespective of the weather. With only one bomb out of seven which left the 'modified' sites during the next few weeks reaching London, the ascendancy gained by the defences became so plain that statements soon appeared in the heavily-censored German press to the effect that the Allies had found a counter-measure to V.1. On August 28 fighters working to seaward of the gun-belt destroyed thirteen of the ninety-seven bombs which approached the country. The gunners accounted for sixty-five, leaving ten to be brought down by fighters over land and nine to continue towards London. Of those nine, two collided with the balloon-barrage, four reached the target, and the remaining three fell short or wide. Significantly, next day Hitler sanctioned an improvised A-4 offensive against London from East Flanders, only to learn within twenty-four hours that no attack could be mounted from an area so far forward.

Thereafter events moved rapidly. Crossing the Seine below Paris on August 29, British and Canadian troops were on the Somme by the last day of the month. Early on September 1 the rear-party of Flakregiment 155 (W) fired their last round from a ramp on French soil before leaving for a camp near Antwerp, whence the regiment moved soon afterwards to Deventer. General Heinemann and the staff of LXV Armee Korps, escaping in the nick of time from the headquarters at Waterloo to which they had retreated earlier from Maisons-Lafitte, moved also to Deventer as British troops were entering Brussels.

The departure of Wachtel's troops from Northern France was followed by a fortnight's lull in the V.1 offensive, briefly interrupted on September 5 when nine missiles approached London from the east. In the early hours of that day III KG.3, a bomber unit which specialised in the air-launching of flying bombs and had aimed about four hundred missiles at London, Southampton and (on one night) Gloucester since the end of the first week in July, made its last effort from bases in Holland before retreating to North-West Germany. Their contribution brought the number of flying bombs aimed at the United Kingdom since the middle of June to about 9,000. Of that total, some 2,000 had crashed soon after launching or otherwise miscarried, leaving 6,725 to reach the English coast or approach it closely enough to come within the ken of the defences. Fighters, guns and the balloon barrage had brought down 3,463, and 2,340 had reached the London Civil Defence Region, in addition to twenty or thirty which reached Portsmouth or Southampton. The weight of high-explosive which fell on London in consequence of Wachtel's efforts and those of III KG.3 between the middle of June and early September was thus about a sixth of the tonnage aimed at the same target by night bombers which flew some eleven thousand sorties for the purpose during the first two months of the 'Blitz' in 1940, and rather more than one-fiftieth of the tonnage aimed by Allied bombers at V.1 targets since December, 1943.

8

False Dawn

I

On June 13, 1944, one of the few A-4 rockets launched at Peenemünde after the opening of the new practice-ground at Blizna went badly astray and fell in Swedish territory near Malmö after a flight of about a hundred miles. Two British intelligence officers whom the Swedish authorities allowed to inspect the remains gave a new slant to Allied thinking by reporting to London that the oxidant carried in the rocket might be liquid oxygen. Arrangements were then made to send the remains to the Royal Aircraft Establishment at Farnborough for detailed examination. The first batch arrived by air towards the middle of July, the last by sea about a fortnight later. On July 31 experts at Farnborough began an attempt to reconstruct the missile.

Many Germans thought it unsporting of the Swedes to betray the secrets of the rocket to the British. The Swedes, on the other hand, may have thought it more than a little careless of the Germans to shoot missiles at them. In the end Hitler consoled himself with the reflection that the Malmö rocket carried a quantity of special equipment and was therefore a misleading specimen.

Meanwhile agents of the Polish intelligence service had transmitted a number of reports from Blizna and had picked up many fragments of fallen missiles, sometimes reaching the spot before the Germans. In July arrangements were made for a key man in the local organisation to convey an oral report to London and take with him as much material as he could carry. He began an adventurous journey by cycling about two hundred miles to a secluded airfield guarded by partisans who declared themselves more than willing to beat off any German patrols which might appear. His arrival was greeted with undisguised relief by the crew of the Allied transport aircraft detailed to pick him up, and by fellow-passengers who could no more afford to be caught trying to leave enemy-held territory than he could. After four unsuccessful attempts and a desperate struggle with a bogged undercarriage in the darkness, the crew at last succeeded in getting the aircraft off the soft surface of the grass airfield, and in due course it landed safely behind the Allied lines in Italy. The Polish emissary reached London on July 28, refused to answer questions before reporting to his superiors, but then confirmed that Dornberger's technicians had been dogged by premature bursts and that the rocket was not yet fit for use.

In the meantime Dr Jones, too, had been through some anxious moments. Coming at the same time as the opening of Wachtel's V.1 offensive, the Malmö incident helped to revive an old fear that long-range rockets might descend on London with little or no warning. Highly placed authorities, aware early in July of widespread dissatisfaction with the Air Ministry's choice of long-range weapon targets, were eager to know what the Air Ministry was doing to discover the secrets of the A-4. The result was that Jones was ordered to report progress at a moment when he knew that he still had much to learn from the Malmö rocket and from the Poles. Foreseeing that even the most cautious attempt to draw conclusions from his existing data might inaugurate an era of wild surmise such as had followed General Nye's unlucky glance at the crystal ball in 1943, he took care to stress in his report the absence of reliable information about such important aspects of the rocket as launching, production and supply. He added, however, that reports from agents who had seen craters in Poland and elsewhere suggested that the war-head might weigh from three to seven tons, and that the missile was manifestly being produced and might therefore come into service in the near future.

Jones's report was circulated on July 16, and thus reached recipients at a moment when some of them were hotly debating the pros and cons of Hill's redistribution of the V.1 defences. Two days later the Prime Minister made one of his rare appearances at a 'Crossbow' meeting, asked whether enough was being done to put all interested parties abreast of developments, and directed that Lord Cherwell should be kept fully in the picture.

On the eve of the next 'Crossbow' meeting a week later, Mr Sandys circulated a report in which he pointed out that the launching-platform for the rocket was now known to be nothing more than an inconspicuous slab of concrete. Adding that the Germans were believed to have made about a thousand rockets, he concluded that an A-4 offensive might be imminent. This conclusion seemed to the Prime Minister and the Minister of Home Security, both of whom attended the 'Crossbow' meeting on July 25, to disclose a threat which ought not to have been allowed to develop without warning.

Backed by Air Chief Marshal Portal and the Secretary of State for Air, Sir Archibald Sinclair, Jones defended himself stoutly against the implied charge that he was a bad watchdog who ought to have barked sooner. He could not argue that the Germans themselves did not expect to begin their offensive before September, for the simple reason that neither he nor anyone in London knew it. What he did say was that no A-4 launching-troops were known to have reached the forward area, that such a move was very unlikely to have taken place without coming to the ears of the War Office and the Air Ministry, and that whether the danger could be described as imminent in the absence of such indications was a matter of opinion. He also pointed out that much of the information on which Mr Sandys relied had only just arrived, and could not, therefore, have been revealed any earlier than Sandys revealed it.

Having thus purchased, not for the first time, his freedom to do his job in his own way, Jones continued his scrutiny of the evidence that was coming in from Farnborough, from Poland and from Allied troops who overran sites and captured documents in Normandy. On August 10, with the reconstruction of the Malmö rocket still in progress, he reported that the rocket weighed about twelve tons and had a one-ton war-head. On August 27 he followed with a comprehensive report which was widely circulated.

Hill and his staff at Stanmore thus became aware by the end of the month of the chief characteristics of the weapon they might have to deal with in succession to the flying bomb or in addition to it. They learned that the rocket was not the sixty-ton monster foreshadowed in earlier reports, that its all-up weight was of the order of twelve to fourteen tons, and that the standard war-head weighed about a ton. It seemed possible, however, that a war-head up to twice as heavy might be fitted at the cost of reducing the normal maximum range of about two hundred miles to perhaps four-fifths of that distance. They learned, too, that storage sites planned by the Germans included underground pits or tunnels, and also wooden bunkers dispersed in woods. They noted that a rocket about to be launched, and the troops launching it, seemed likely to be vulnerable to air attack during a period of perhaps two hours while the missile, standing upright on its launching-platform, was being fuelled and made ready for despatch. Finally, they took note of indications that active operations might begin during the first half of September.

At that stage, however, what seemed to be a tolerably clear

prospect became confused as a result of the swiftness of the British advance from the Seine through North-East France and into Belgium. A lively hope that the left flank of the Allied armies would continue without check through Holland and into Germany, capturing all possible launching-areas for long-range weapons as it went, was dimmed when the Supreme Commander refused to go the whole way with the British idea that he should halt his right and strike with his left; but it was not finally extinguished until the failure of the stop-gap Arnhem operation left the Allies bogged down for the winter. One consequence was that, from the British point of view, the later stages of the V.1 offensive became almost as closely linked with the development of the V.2 offensive as the search for the 'air mine with wings' was with the search for the rocket in 1943.

II

From the moment when the A-4 emerged from the development stage, the SS showed a strong inclination to adopt so promising a weapon as their own. When the Führer ruled after Bomber Command's attack on Peenemünde in August, 1943, that a high proportion of trial launchings should be made in an area safe from air attack, Blizna was chosen largely because the SS had a suitable site there. Similarly, the transfer of assembly to Niedersachswerfen, also a place in which the SS were interested, gave the SS leaders some degree of control over production. Eventually many components of the rocket were not merely assembled at Niedersachswerfen, but made there.

As long as the German Army remained outwardly loyal, Hitler seems not to have contemplated removing the A-4 from their control so far as technical development and operations in the field were concerned. After his attempted assassination in July, 1944, however, he took the significant step of appointing the notorious Heinrich Himmler Special Commissioner for

THE GERMAN LONG-RANGE ROCKET
ORGANISATION

This diagram shows the *de facto* A-4 organisation early in September, 1944, when active operations began with the SS in control and LXV Armee Korps no longer in the A-4 picture. It will be seen that the strength deployed against all targets (five batteries) was less than the equivalent of two complete *Abteilungen*.

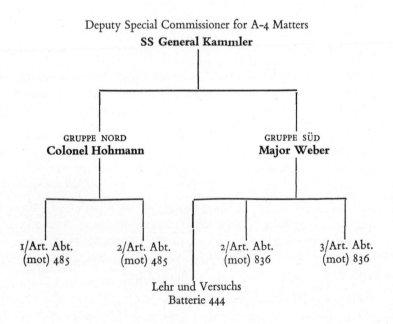

Deputy Special Commissioner for A-4 Matters
SS General Kammler

GRUPPE NORD	GRUPPE SÜD
Colonel Hohmann	**Major Weber**

1/Art. Abt.	2/Art. Abt.		2/Art. Abt.	3/Art. Abt.
(mot) 485	(mot) 485		(mot) 836	(mot) 836

Lehr und Versuchs
Batterie 444

A-4 Matters. The appointment was made on August 6, less than three weeks after the attempt on Hitler's life.

It was therefore with Himmler's deputy, SS General Kammler, in the background that Hitler sanctioned, on August 29, a projected A-4 offensive against London from the area between Tournai and Ghent. On the same day the British began their advance across the Seine, and on the next the neighbourhood of Antwerp and Malines was substituted for the Ghent-Tournai area as a suitable location for the launching-troops. Simultaneously, Heinemann dropped out of the chain of command, with the result that the way was left clear to Kammler, although ostensibly the effect was to give Metz an independent command.

The Allied advance was so rapid that no more was heard of an offensive from Antwerp-Malines. Nor does anything more appear to have been heard of Metz. By the end of August Kammler was established at Cleve, north-west of the Ruhr. A few days later he moved forward to Berg en Del, on Dutch soil near Nijmegen. Meanwhile the launching-troops, some six thousand strong and equipped with nearly sixteen hundred vehicles, were moving in two groups into Western Germany and Holland. Two batteries comprising Gruppe Nord (Colonel Hohmann) assembled near Cleve; the two batteries of Gruppe Süd (Major Weber) advanced from the Rhineland to the neighbourhood of Venlo, but afterwards recrossed the frontier and took up a position near Euskirchen. On September 5 Kammler ordered Gruppe Nord to The Hague for an offensive against London, and Gruppe Süd to prepare for attacks on targets in France and Belgium. At the same time he attached an experimental and demonstration battery to Gruppe Süd for the special purpose of attacking Paris.

Either these moves were not reported at the time by Allied intelligence sources, or their significance was not understood in London. Dr Jones had argued convincingly in July that the

NORTH

SEA

Terschelling

Zuider Zee

Sneek

Staveren

Zwolle

Amsterdam

Leiden

THE HAGUE

Loosduinen

Apeldoorn

Arnhem

Darfeld

Münster

Rotterdam

Alblasserdam

Nijmegen

Cleve

Berg-en-Del

R. Rhine

Walcheren

Flushing

Venlo

Düsseldorf

Bruges

Antwerp

Ghent

Malines

Cologne

BRUSSELS

Maastricht

Tournai

Liége

Euskirchen

⌐ General Kammler's Headquarters until Sept. 17

⌐ General Kammler's Headquarters after Sept. 17

⬭ Areas from which rockets were aimed at U.K.

0   50   100

MILES

EDGAR HOLLOWAY

V.2 ORGANISATION IN HOLLAND: SEPTEMBER 1944

Germans could not have moved their A-4 launching-troops into France without attracting notice; to know early in September what might be happening to such relatively obscure formations on the far side of the Rhine or the Meuse was another matter.

The result was that, in the absence of reliable indications of the enemy's intentions, the attitude of the Vice-Chiefs and Chiefs of Staff to the prospect of further long-range attacks on London changed with startling abruptness as the Allied armies surged forward in France and Belgium.

During the last week in August, no one acquainted with the current intelligence picture would have dissented from the proposition that the A-4 rocket was likely to go into service during the first half of September, that the Germans would then be free to launch missiles aimed at London from inconspicuous platforms in any part of Europe within two hundred miles which they might still hold, and that such platforms could be as easily constructed in one country as in another. Nor would anyone have denied that air-launched flying bombs could still reach London even if all Wachtel's ramps were captured, or that the range of the bomb might conceivably be increased. As late as the last few days of the month the Chiefs of Staff urged Hill to send fighters on armed reconnaissance over France and Flanders on the ground that 'the stage of imminent attack' with long-range rockets was at hand, and Harris to bomb suspected rocket-stores in Northern France. Yet only a few days later they were declaring that rocket attacks on London need no longer be expected, and were encouraging Mr Sandys, in effect if not expressly, to tell the world that the Battle of London was over 'except possibly for a few last shots'

On August 30 Hill's fighters did begin to fly armed reconnaissance sorties as proposed. Five days later the sorties had to be discontinued because the whole of the area they covered was either in Allied hands or within the zone reserved for the tactical air forces. Hill then learned that the Chiefs of Staff considered that the threat to London from long-range rockets had passed. His staff warned him that they could not reconcile that conclusion with what they knew of the weapon, and that rockets seemed to them quite likely to be aimed at London within the next ten days from Western Holland. Hill was glad to hear next day that a review of the situation by the Vice-Chiefs had led the Chiefs of Staff to conclude that his radar watch for rockets ought to be kept up, not so much because they thought that his intelligence officers were right and they themselves were wrong, as because it seemed to them possible that targets other than London might be attacked.

As it happened, this last exchange took place on the day which opened with the launching of a few flying bombs by III KG.3 before that unit left its Dutch bases for North-West Germany. The very fact that the unit was known soon after-wards to be departing tended, however, to strengthen an impression that the German long-range weapon organisation was breaking up. Even if it were not, there seemed little reason to doubt that the V.1 offensive, at any rate, was over, at least for the time being. Although Hill's staff did not share the hopeful-ness of the Chiefs of Staff where long-range rockets were con-cerned, even they might have found it hard to believe on September 5 that not only more than fourteen hundred long-range rockets, but also more than fourteen hundred flying bombs, would be aimed at the United Kingdom during the next six or seven months.

9

The Double Threat

In accordance with the orders given by Kammler on September 6, Gruppe Nord moved between that day and September 8 to The Hague for the purpose of opening attacks on London. The first use of the A-4 rocket in active operations, at any rate so far as the Western theatre was concerned, was made, however, by the experimental battery attached to Gruppe Süd. After two unsuccessful attempts on September 6, the experimental battery succeeded in landing a rocket on a Paris suburb early on September 8, but afterwards moved from the Rhineland to Walcheren with the object of augmenting the effort against London.

At 6.43 p.m. that evening, Londoners whom five years of war had made familiar with sudden noises were only mildly startled by a sound which resembled a sharp clap of thunder. At that moment a rocket launched from The Hague about five minutes earlier fell at Chiswick, killing three people and seriously injuring another ten. Sixteen seconds later a second rocket despatched from the same quarter demolished some wooden huts near Epping, but did no other damage and caused no casualties.

So far as the air defence commander was concerned, the immediate consequence of these events was that henceforth he faced the problem not only of defending the country against any revival of the V.1 offensive which the enemy might have in view, but also of providing such means of defence as might be possible against V.2. Since the arrival of the first two rockets coincided fairly closely with the move of Leigh-Mallory's main headquarters to the Continent, the air defence commander was saddled, too, with at least nominal responsibility for co-ordinating offensive counter-measures to both weapons.

Hill had no offensive resources of his own, except insofar as fighters might be used offensively, nor had he the power to order the commanders of the heavy bomber and tactical bomber forces to attack targets of his choosing. He knew that he could not hope to do more than invite them to attack such targets, and afterwards make representations to higher authority if they failed to comply. He also knew that the Air Ministry would be reluctant to give any but very broad directives to operational commanders.

In any case, the first thing was to find out where the rockets were coming from. For that purpose a number of stations were keeping a special radar watch for rockets rising from enemy-held territory, and the 11th Survey Regiment, Royal Artillery, with headquarters at Canterbury, was keeping a parallel watch with sound-ranging and flash-spotting equipment. All these arrangements had been made on the assumption that rockets would come, if they came at all, from the south or south-east rather than the east, and the equipment had been sited accordingly. Even so, it provided data accurate enough to confirm the fairly obvious assumption that the first two rockets to arrive had been launched from South-West Holland, and within a few hours some of Hill's aircraft were on their way to that area to see what they could see.

During the next few days Hill arranged to double the number of stations between Dover and Lowestoft which kept a special radar watch for ascending rockets, and the 11th Survey Regiment acquired a number of observation balloons to increase the effective range of its equipment. He also arranged to deploy mobile radar stations and the 10th Survey Regiment on the Continent, the whole forming an outpost of his command and reporting to him through No. 105 Mobile Air Reporting Unit, set up for the purpose with headquarters at Malines.

At any rate in the early stages, data from radar stations and sound-ranging and flash-spotting units a long way from the launching-area proved too imprecise to pinpoint launching-sites, although it did give a rough indication of their where-abouts. On the other hand, the sight and sound of a rocket rising under the impetus of a 25-ton thrust, and belching forth flames and clouds of smoke, could not be hidden from observers near the spot. Almost from the beginning members of the Dutch resistance movement, briefed from London, transmitted a stream of information about the activities of the launching-units at The Hague, and also a much smaller number of reports which threw a rather uncertain light on those of the experimental battery, which began to aim rockets at London on September 14. Means were found of getting reports of launchings to London almost immediately after the observations were made, and they were then passed to Hill's headquarters, where one of his intelligence officers correlated them with the technical data from radar, sound-ranging and flash-spotting units. In this way Hill was able to ensure after the first day or two that pilots sent on armed reconnaissance were briefed to visit groups of known sites which could be reckoned in current use, inasmuch as rockets appeared to have been launched from them within the last day or so or even within the last few hours.

The weakness of armed reconnaissance as a counter-measure to the rocket was, however, that even the most up-to-the-minute information could not give the pilots more than an outside chance of finding a particular site actually in use at the moment of their arrival. Unless a rocket was being placed in position or fuelled and serviced, there would be nothing to see and nothing to attack, except that troops and vehicles might be encountered more or less fortuitously. From the beginning, therefore, Hill was attracted by the idea of destroying stores or cutting communications. Reports from Dutch informants mentioned three suburban properties, all more or less heavily wooded, where rockets were thought to be stored, and some of them also mentioned 'bunkers' which sounded very much like the 'wooden bunkers dispersed in woods' which the Germans were believed to have planned in France. One of these properties, called Raaphorst, was fairly large, and the exact location of any bunkers there was not clear. At the other two, Ter Horst and Eikenhorst, the wooded parts were small enough to give a reasonable chance that a moderate bomb-load aimed at them would settle the hash of any rockets they might hold. Accordingly, Hill asked Bomber Command to attack Ter Horst and Eikenhorst. Without waiting for Hill's request, Air Chief Marshal Harris sent a small force to Raaphorst on September 14, but three days later he duly attacked Eikenhorst. Having taken on two A-4 targets within a space of a few days, he was not prepared to tackle a third for the moment, and so Ter Horst went unscathed.

Thus the position as seen from Hill's headquarters a week after the first rocket fell at Chiswick was that no flying bombs had reached the country for more than ten days. About two hundred heavy and nearly six hundred light guns deployed round the Thames Estuary in recent months to guard London against air-launched bombs approaching from the east were, however, still in position, since the Chiefs of Staff agreed with Hill that to do away with them would be rash. On the other hand, rockets were arriving at the rate of about two a day, although not all were reaching London. Energetic measures were being taken to make the radar and counter-observation watch for rockets more effective, not least because in time it might become the basis of a public warning system. A valuable but by no means complete picture of German activities at The

Hague had been built up, and Hill's fighters were making armed reconnaissances of the area at the rate of about a hundred sorties a day. Finally, Bomber Command had attacked Raaphorst without being asked to do so, and were soon to attack Eikenhorst at Hill's request. Short of a massive programme of bombing which Hill had no chance of carrying out, no effective counter-measure to the long-range rocket was in sight; but it was encouraging that the weapon was proving much less formidable than was expected at one time, and that hitherto casualties had been very light.

Such was the picture on the evening of September 15. Towards dawn on September 16, III KG.3 introduced a new feature by resuming air-launching, but this time aiming their missiles at London from the north-east. This was not altogether unexpected, but it was disturbing because it suggested that the enemy might be alive to the possibility of not only outflanking the defences to the north by successive stages, but also varying the direction of his attacks so that the defenders were kept guessing. Hill and Pile had already been forced, in effect, to divert part of their resources from the gun-belt on the South Coast in order to provide the seven or eight hundred guns round the Thames Estuary, thus creating a 'Diver Box' as well as a 'Diver Belt'. They responded to the new move by adding a 'Diver Strip' between Clacton and Yarmouth, but the process could not be continued indefinitely, even though it was possible to withdraw a good many guns from the South Coast without much risk. Should the enemy exploit to the full the mobility of his air-launching unit they might face awkward problems, since they could not put guns everywhere along the coast without making the defences too thin to be effective. What, however, they could do, and did, was to draw up provisional schemes for likely stretches of coast and likely targets.

About fifteen Heinkel 111 aircraft of III KG.3 took part in the first bout of the new phase, and launched at least nine flying bombs. Two of the missiles were shot down by ships at sea. Of the remaining seven which came within the ken of the defences, fighters brought down three, two went far astray, and the other two fell in the built-up area of London at Barking and Woolwich.

Next day the Allies began their attempt to get a footing across the Lower Rhine and Maas with the help of a large-scale airborne operation. Himself withdrawing to Darfeld, near Münster, Kammler ordered Gruppe Nord to Burgsteinfurt, also in that area, and the experimental battery to Zwolle. In the course of the day Dutch informants reported that the launching-troops were leaving The Hague, but at least some troops remained in the forward area as late as the evening of September 18, when they brought off an exceptionally accurate shot by landing a rocket at Lambeth, about a mile from the government quarter between Whitehall and St James's Park which the German High Command presumably had in mind when they gave as the aiming-point for all rounds a position roughly a thousand yards east of Waterloo Station. Up to the time of their withdrawal Gruppe Nord and the experimental battery had aimed about thirty-five rockets at London. Of the twenty-seven which flew far enough for their fate to be recorded, sixteen fell in the London Civil Defence Region, six in Essex, two in Sussex, one on a mud-flat in the Thames Estuary, and the remaining two in the sea off Shoeburyness and Clacton.

On the evening of September 17 III KG.3 again took up the V.1 offensive after an interval which gave General Pile a chance to start moving guns to their new positions in the 'Strip'. Further launchings followed on most nights during the rest of the month and on many nights thereafter.

As long as the enemy relied on air-launching, Hill could reasonably hope to keep down the number of bombs reaching London both by shooting down the missiles and by shooting down the aircraft which launched them. Neither proved particularly easy. To escape detection, the launching-aircraft flew only a few hundred feet above the surface of the sea, rising to a height of two thousand feet or so to release their missiles. The radar-sets carried by Hill's night-fighters did not work well at such low altitudes. Moreover, his night-fighter crews were accustomed to a system of close control from ground stations which was not designed to meet such conditions. Besides modifying the equipment of a number of stations, Hill experimented with control from a naval frigate and from a Wellington aircraft equipped with air-to-surface-vessel radar, but some time elapsed before these innovations brought much benefit. On the other hand, the work was so hazardous for the launching-crews that shooting down their aircraft would have been almost superfluous if the Luftwaffe had not been prepared to accept poor results and heavy losses for the sake of keeping the offensive alive. Of the forty-one launching-aircraft lost by the Germans on operational flights in the autumn and early winter, probably not more than half were destroyed by the bull-dog persistence of Hill's Mosquito crews, the rest succumbing to accidents of one kind or another.

Shooting down the missiles themselves was also difficult for both guns and fighters. It was difficult for the guns because the bombs flew even lower than those launched from ramps, often whizzing through the field of fire at a thousand feet or so. This meant that equipment had to be so sited as to give the best results against low-flying targets even at the cost of still further reducing the length of the warning which gunners could hope to get. Another difficulty was that priority had often to be given to Allied bombers coming and going over the North Sea, so that the gunners in the 'Strip' did not have the same freedom of fire as those on the South Coast and round the Thames Estuary. In spite of these handicaps the gunners performed outstandingly, shooting down more than half the bombs which escaped fighters and naval gunfire to seaward of them.

The chief problem for fighter-pilots working in front of the 'Strip' and over the land behind it was the difficulty which most of them had in judging their distance from the target. The tongue of flame emitted by a flying bomb was plainly visible in the darkness, but pilots had to estimate its range before they could open fire with any prospect of success. Sir Thomas Merton, a distinguished scientist, was brought in to devise a simple range-finder to which Hill gave high praise, but big variations between individual scores showed that personal skill was still the decisive factor.

As with V.2, Hill's thoughts turned to offensive action. The air-launching unit was known or believed to be using four aerodromes at Varrelbusch, Zwischenahn, Aalhorn and Handorf-bei-Münster. The Chiefs of Staff agreed early in September that these should be attacked in the course of a general offensive against the Luftwaffe by the Allied bomber forces. Handorf was in fact bombed several times in late September and early October by Bomber Command and the United States Eighth Air Force, but bad weather spoiled a projected attack on a whole group of aerodromes in North-West Germany which was to have included Varrelbusch and Zwischenahn. Warned by intelligence sources a little later that the air-launching unit was likely to expand, Hill pressed Bomber Command and the Air Ministry to do more, but the response was not encouraging. During the autumn and early winter III KG.3 was duly reinforced at the expense of moribund bomber units, ultimately attaining the status of a full Geschwader with the designation KG.53.

II

A few days after its move from Walcheren, Kammler ordered

the experimental battery to keep the V.2 offensive going by moving to Staveren, in Friesland, and opening fire on Norwich and Ipswich. The new phase began at 7.10 p.m. on September 25, when a rocket fell at Hoxne in Suffolk. Between that date and October 12 the battery aimed forty-three rounds at Norwich and one at Ipswich. Thirty-two rockets came down in England, five were seen to fall into the sea, and the other seven failed to arrive within sight of the United Kingdom. No hits were scored on either target, but one round fell in the outskirts of Norwich although outside the city boundary. Many of the rockets fell harmlessly in open country, and casualties were very light.

At first Hill's staff were not sure whether the rockets were coming from Friesland or from the neighbourhood of Apeldoorn, but at any rate it was clear that their source was too remote to be efficiently covered by fighters from England. Accordingly the Second Tactical Air Force assumed responsibility for armed reconnaissance and were fed from Stanmore with all the information Hill's intelligence officers could collect. Almost simultaneously news was received that such places as Liége and Brussels were being bombarded with rockets and were likely to become targets for flying bombs launched from ramps in Western Germany. Ultimately Antwerp became the chief Continental target for V-weapons, and the only Continental target for V.2.

To meet this new development, Hill provided the nucleus of an organisation established at Versailles to keep the Supreme Commander abreast of the situation in his command, and parted with No. 105 Mobile Air Reporting Unit and the 11th Survey Regiment for his benefit. At the same time the 10th Survey Regiment returned to normal duties in the field, thus dropping out of the V.2 picture. These arrangements were acceptable to Hill, not only because he recognised the Supreme Commander's prior claim but also because the experience of the last few weeks suggested that he could do without a survey regiment in Kent as long as he maintained his radar watch on the East Coast and kept in touch with his other sources of information.

By the end of September, however, the failure of the Allied airborne operation at Arnhem and Nijmegen had become apparent to the Germans, and on the last day of the month Kammler ordered one battery of Gruppe Nord to return to The Hague and resume the attack on London. On October 3 warning was received at Hill's headquarters that the launching-troops were coming back, and late that evening a rocket fell at Leytonstone, about seven miles north-east of the centre of London. By the middle of the month rockets were reaching the United Kingdom at the rate of about two or three a day, and the enemy was said to be about to reinforce the launching-troops at The Hague, as in fact he did a week later.

Soon after the resumption of V.2 attacks on London, Leigh-Mallory ruled that it did not affect the responsibility of the Second Tactical Air Force for armed reconnaissance of launching-areas. This was unsatisfactory to Hill, who found himself responsible for defending the country against rockets, yet powerless to order bombers to attack supplies and communications, and now equally powerless to use his own fighters to harass launching-crews.

Fortunately for his peace of mind, the knot was soon untied. On October 15 the Allied Expeditionary Air Force was disbanded, Air Defence of Great Britain became Fighter Command, and Hill achieved independence as Commander-in-Chief. He was then able to make a new bargain with the Second Tactical Air Force, Supreme Headquarters, and the Air Ministry. Henceforth Fighter Command would take care of launching-areas so placed that rockets coming from them were likely to be aimed at the United Kingdom; the Second Tactical Air Force of sites which threatened Continental targets. Air

Marshal Coningham of the Second Tactical Air Force agreed to cover The Hague on days when the weather was such that Hill's fighters could not operate but his could.

These arrangements helped to smooth the way for the transfer of No. 105 Mobile Air Reporting Unit and the 11th Survey Regiment to the Supreme Commander's control, and their only unsatisfactory feature was that Hill still had no promise that any of the targets he had proposed to the bomber forces would be attacked. His position at the end of October was that he had asked Bomber Command to tackle three air-launching bases in North-West Germany, and two V.2 targets at The Hague which were so close together that, in effect, they formed a single complex. With Coningham's assent, he had also asked No. 2 Group, one of Coningham's subordinate formations, to take on three V.2 targets which seemed to call for the 'bomb-trickling' treatment in which No. 2 Group specialised. Air Chief Marshal Harris's staff agreed with Hill's that the air-launching bases were acceptable targets, but were not prepared to commit their chief beyond that point. No. 2 Group, on the other hand, regarded the targets proposed to them as unsuitable. In general, the view taken outside Hill's headquarters was that the tactical bomber forces were already maintaining an energetic offensive against German communications, and that further offensive measures were hardly needed to counter V.1 and V.2 offensives which seemed unlikely to become a serious menace to the home country. Against Hill's fear that the 'Diver' defences might be outflanked and the rocket offensive grow could be balanced the solid fact that only a sprinkling of flying bombs and about a hundred and twenty rockets had reached the United Kingdom in the last two months.

10

The Last Months

I

On the whole, the British public found V.2 a less alarming weapon than V.1. This was partly, of course, because far fewer rockets than flying bombs reached the country, but it was also partly because the rocket arrived unheralded by the dismal rattle of the bomb, and often unnoticed by people outside the immediate vicinity of the point of impact. During the lull which followed the first bout of firing at London, the Chiefs of Staff recommended that no public announcement about Hitler's new weapon should be made for the time being. They also came to the conclusion that, at any rate for the present, any attempt to warn the public of the approach of individual rockets would lead to many false warnings and the arrival of at least some rockets without notice. The result was that each missile came as a bolt from the blue which made little impression on members of the public not immediately concerned.

Another factor which helped to make V.2 less disturbing than V.1 to the peace of mind of the ordinary citizen was that damage done by the rocket was confined, as a rule, to a comparatively small area. Even though the rocket's passage through the atmosphere slowed it from its maximum velocity of 3,600 miles an hour to roughly two-thirds of that speed immediately before impact, it was still travelling so fast up to the last moment that the war-head, relatively coarsely fused to reduce the risk of premature bursts, tended to plough into the ground before exploding. In broad terms, each flying bomb which eluded the defences and came down on land killed or seriously injured between six and seven people; but in addition almost every one which fell in a densely-populated neighbourhood inflicted minor injuries, broke windows, wrenched off tiles, and defaced brickwork over a wide radius. In the London suburb of Croydon, for example, a hundred and forty flying bombs damaged or destroyed three out of four houses in the borough. Each rocket down on land killed or seriously injured between eight and nine people, but minor injuries and superficial damage were much less widespread. In a sense the average householder, to whom possessions as well as life were dear, thus had less cause to dread the rocket than the bomb.

In the early stages of the V.1 offensive the authorities noticed not only a marked exodus from London of people who could get away, but also a bigger decline in the output of some factories than could be attributed merely to the time lost when workers took shelter in consequence of the sounding of air-raid warnings at the beginning of each bout. Production suffered because efficiency was undermined by lack of sleep, and also because occupants of damaged houses tended to stay away for a shift or two while the household was getting on its feet again. These troubles began to mend as local warning-systems and emergency repair services improved and when doodle-bugs ceased to be a novelty; but a still more significant trend was the return to London of voluntary absentees. Even before the end of Wachtel's V.1 attacks from Northern France, Londoners who had taken refuge in the country in the early summer were beginning to come back. In the autumn and early winter the influx continued at such a rate that by the end of the year more than nine-tenths had either returned or been replaced by newcomers or by exiles of longer standing.

When the trend began it could be interpreted as a heartening sign of confidence in the ability of the air defences to get the better of the bomb, or perhaps in that of the Allied armies to capture the launching-area without delay. By October it had come to have an embarrassing side for both the air defence commander and the Minister of Home Security. After Kammler's reinforcement of the V.2 launching-troops at The Hague the scale of attack on London began to rise. Almost simultaneously the enemy's fire became more accurate, supposedly because the troops were growing more experienced, perhaps also because a method of avoiding deterioration during storage by taking missiles straight from the assembly-plant to the forward area was introduced about that time. In nine days at the end of October and early in November forty-four rockets reached the country. Forty fell in the London Civil Defence Region or elsewhere within twenty-five miles of Charing Cross, and their mean point of impact was in Poplar, less than six miles east of the government quarter and at the heart of an important dockland area. Two rockets which fell at Camberwell and Deptford on November 1 killed or seriously injured more than a hundred and twenty people. A week later the German authorities announced publicly that the V.2 offensive had begun.

In order not to give the enemy any indication of the accuracy of his fire, the Prime Minister did not mention London when he confirmed on November 10 that the country was under bombardment with long-range rockets. The Germans succeeded in getting a certain amount of information about the effects of their attacks, but some of it was misleading. Their general impression seems to have been that they were doing much better than they really were.

Even so, casualties in the last week of October and the first three weeks of November were many times heavier than in the whole of the preceding period since September 8. Hill pressed once more for attacks by heavy bombers on V.2 targets, but again without success, the Chiefs of Staff and others arguing that the diversion of part of Bomber Command's effort from other objectives would be strategically unsound, and that such attacks would bring heavy loss of life among Dutch civilians. Pointing out that the enemy's policy seemed to be to turn civilians out of buildings occupied by his troops, Hill asked that at least he should be allowed to make fighter-bomber attacks on the sites, using his own fighters in that role as he had already done in areas away from buildings. He suggested that representatives of the Netherlands government in London should be consulted, and that they might be asked to weigh the risk to civilians in their own country against the certain loss of life in England.

A powerful argument in Hill's favour was that Dutchmen and Dutchwomen at The Hague and elsewhere, not all of them members of the resistance movement, showed a touching eagerness to help by putting their local knowledge at the disposal of the Allies, well knowing that the effect might be to call down attacks on their capital. About the end of the third week in November spokesmen of the Netherlands government agreed to raise no immediate objection to attacks on the lines proposed, stipulating only that Hill should satisfy himself that the attacks were necessary and likely to prove effective, and that he should show 'reasonable discrimination'. Towards the end of the month Hill's fighter-bombers began a new programme of attacks on targets in built-up areas from which civilians were known to have been removed. In the first three days they made rather more than a hundred sorties and dropped about ten tons of bombs.

The Minister of Home Security also asked that part of the heavy bomber force should be switched to V.2 targets, but was no more successful than Hill. Mr Morrison's great fear was that, if the offensive were allowed to go unchecked, sooner or later a rocket would go through one of the tunnels under the Thames. Water sweeping into one or more of the tube-stations on either side of the river might then drown thousands of men, women and children who spent their nights there, many of them more from force of habit and because they liked the warmth and company than because they expected to be bombed if they stayed above ground. Flood-gates, first put in hand about the time of Munich, had been built to guard against penetration of the tunnels by bombs dropped from aircraft, but they were closed only when warning of an impending air raid was received.

The sequel was a scheme by which a warning was passed from the operations room at Stanmore to the London Passenger Transport Board whenever radar stations detected a rocket rising from The Hague. It worked well for the purpose in view, but would not have made a satisfactory basis for a public warning system, since many rockets detected by radar failed to arrive, and not all those which did arrive reached London. If the maroons tentatively installed when counter-measures were first considered had been let off every time an ascending rocket was detected, there would have been so many false alarms that confidence in the system would soon have been undermined, although that would not have prevented people outside London from complaining that they were left out in the cold.

This was not the only argument against public warnings. An equally strong one was that the rocket took only about five minutes to cover the two hundred miles from The Hague to London. Thus the effect of firing maroons even at the earliest possible moment would be to arouse painful apprehensions without giving more than a few fortunately-placed people time to take any useful action. Another point was that no ordinary shelter was proof against a direct hit, and that the danger from anything but a direct hit was comparatively small.

The fact remained that the early winter found the air defence commander with no sure hope of preventing the enemy from

V.1 in flight.

Fighter *versus* V.1.

V.1 diving on central London.

V.1 storage depot at Saint-Leu-d'Esserent (from a painting by
Graham Sutherland).

Air Chief Marshal Sir Trafford Leigh-Mallory.

Roderic Hill.

General Carl Spaatz.

Lieutenant-General Sir Frederick Pile, Bt.

Constance Babington Smith.

Lieutenant-General Ira Eaker.

Air photograph of Bois Carré site after Allied bombing.

V.2 shortly before launching.

V.2 leaving launching platform.

increasing the scale of his attack if he had the will and the means
to do so, and the Minister of Home Security powerless to do
more than guard against the worst consequences of unlucky
hits. Their consolation was the knowledge that the attitude of
the Chiefs of Staff, the Air Ministry and Supreme Headquarters to the use of the bomber forces was likely to change
abruptly if anything disastrous happened. By that time a good
many people would have been killed and they themselves
might be out of their jobs; but such was war.

II

On November 25, only a few days after Hill had pleaded for
attacks on V.2 targets by heavy bombers, a rocket struck a
crowded building in the New Cross Road, between four and
five miles south-east of Whitehall. Two hundred and sixty-
eight people were killed or seriously injured. This was by far
the largest number of casualties yet caused by a single rocket;
but any hope which Hill may have had that the transformation
which followed Wachtel's hit on the Royal Military Chapel
in June would be repeated proved vain. The two incidents
were set apart not only by the difference between four or five
miles and a quarter of a mile, but also by the disparity between
Wachtel's hundred missiles a day and Kammler's six or seven.
The determination of the Chiefs of Staff and the Supreme
Commander to give only a low priority to the bombing of
rocket-sites remained unshaken, and Hill was left to do the best
he could with his own resources.

In December his fighter-bombers flew nearly four hundred
sorties over The Hague, and aimed more than forty tons of
bombs at targets all at least 250 yards from the nearest building
known to be still housing Dutch civilians. Probably the most
successful of these operations was an attack by thirty-three
Spitfires of No. 299 Squadron, No. 602 (City of Glasgow)

Squadron, and No. 453 (Royal Australian Air Force) Squadron on a block of flats in which rocket-troops were housed. German casualties were light, but the place was badly knocked about and the troops were afterwards reported to have left it.

To all appearances the attacks had a salutary effect. The number of rockets reaching the United Kingdom fell from an average of seven a day at the end of November to four a day in the middle of December, and for some weeks most launchings were made at night. This was a benefit, inasmuch as casualties were usually lighter after dark; but the trend was not maintained. In the first half of January the number of rockets reaching the country rose again to an average of eight a day, and soon the Germans were making more than half their launchings in daylight.

Meanwhile Hill's prediction that the 'Diver' defences might be outflanked was fulfilled. Towards dawn on December 24 about fifty aircraft of KG.53 aimed flying bombs at Manchester from points off the East Coast between Skegness and Bridlington. The thirty bombs which reached the coast crossed it well north of the 'Strip', and none was shot down although the Humber defences opened fire at seven missiles which passed over their area. Only one bomb reached Manchester, but six fell within ten miles and more than a hundred people were killed or seriously injured. Within a few hours Hill ordered the immediate deployment of sixty heavy guns between Skegness and Filey as the first instalment of a northward extension of the 'Strip' which he and Pile called the 'Fringe'. The strength of the 'Fringe' rose to eighty-eight heavy and sixteen light guns by the end of January, and further additions were made later. Provision was made to raise the number of heavy guns in the 'Fringe' to 212 in case of need, and schemes were also drawn up for the Tyne, Tees, Forth and Clyde.

But the sands were running out for KG.53. Towards the middle of January Kammler added effective control of V.1 to the grip he already had on V.2. On the ground that KG.53's bases might soon become untenable, and perhaps also because the Luftwaffe was short of high-grade aviation spirit though not of the lower-grade fuel used in the bombs themselves, he decided almost at once to suspend air-launchings. No more attacks were made on Manchester, and at 2.13 a.m. on January 14 the last air-launched flying bomb to reach the United Kingdom fell at Hornsey, in the northern outskirts of London.

Since September 16 about 1,200 bombs, all air-launched, had been aimed at the country, but only 638 had come near enough to be observed by the defences. Guns and fighters had brought down 403, leaving sixty-six to reach the London Civil Defence Region, one to reach Manchester, and 168 to fall elsewhere. This was a remarkable achievement on the part of the air defences, whose triumph over the ground-launched bomb in August had already been recognised in a formal letter of approbation with which the Air Ministry did their best to soften any hard feelings left by their brush with Hill when he moved the gun-belt.

For the next six weeks or so rockets alone continued to arrive, the number rising in the middle of February to an average of ten a day. In the meantime Hill raised the strength of his special fighter-bomber force from four to six squadrons at the request of the Air Ministry, who promised in return that the Second Tactical Air Force should be asked to make a substantial contribution.

What form that contribution should take was not an easy question to answer in view of Air Marshal Coningham's dismissal of the targets proposed by Hill. One suggestion which Coningham did adopt was that he should bear in mind the location of rocket-sites when planning his programme of attacks on communications. As early as December, however, the Air Ministry had decided on a new approach. They asked the Foreign Office and the Ministry of Economic Warfare to look into the chances of starving the launching-troops of liquid oxygen by destroying their sources of supply. Confessing that they had no means of knowing from which of many possible sources the troops at The Hague were drawing their quota, the experts did their best to oblige by listing eight factories in Holland and ten in Germany which might fill the bill. Coningham was prevailed upon to attack one of the Dutch factories on January 22, and early in February Hill reluctantly tackled a second, so awkwardly situated that his fighter-bombers had to make five separate attacks in order to minimise damage to adjacent property while giving themselves a fair chance of damaging the target. The bombing of these two factories had no discoverable effect on the enemy's rate of fire, nor did it seem likely to have any while so many other sources of liquid oxygen remained open.

Altogether, the fighter-bombers made 1,143 sorties against rocket-targets in the first two months of 1945 and dropped 216 tons of bombs. About the middle of February Hill's Chief Intelligence Officer, Group Captain Vorley Harris, suggested that they should try concentrating their whole effort on a single target for at least some days at a time. The target chosen for the experiment was the Haagsche Bosch, a wooded, park-like area where up to twenty to thirty rockets at a time had been seen on air photographs since December. As the sequel to thirty-eight attacks delivered on February 21 and 22, air photographs taken on February 24 showed no rockets at the Haagsche Bosch, but up to six were seen close by in an open space at Duindigt. The attacks were followed by a lull of more than sixty hours during which only one rocket reached the country.

In the light of this evidence and of other indications that the launching-troops were taking up new positions, the Haagsche Bosch as such was removed on March 1 from the target-list periodically circulated to all concerned. Its place at the top of the list was taken by a new target comprising part of Duindigt and that part of the Haagsche Bosch immediately next to it. The rest of Duindigt took second place.

It was therefore surprising that when, on March 3, the Second Tactical Air Force at last made a direct contribution to the offensive against the rocket-launching organisation, the target they chose was neither of these but the Haagsche Bosch itself. Worse still, an incorrect allowance for wind led to many casualties among Dutch civilians. Not one bomb fell within five hundred yards of the selected aiming-points, and a great part of the bomb-load fell in a densely-populated area about a mile away. An understandable consequence was that Coningham became more reluctant than ever to have anything to do with rocket-targets.

On the same day the struggle against V.1 entered a new phase, which proved to be its last. In February the Germans were known to be developing a new version of the flying bomb capable of reaching London from sites in Western Holland. Accordingly a search for such sites was begun. On February 26 photographic interpreters found sites aligned on London at Ypenburg, near The Hague, and Vlaardingen, near Rotterdam, but missed a third site near Delft. The Germans had also built three sites aligned on Antwerp. No immediate steps were taken to attack the sites, but Hill and Pile at once arranged to reinforce the 'Diver' defences between Sheppey and Orfordness by removing twelve eight-gun heavy batteries from the northern part of the 'Strip' and moving in six new batteries as a partial replacement. In addition Hill earmarked three Mustang squadrons to patrol to seaward of the guns and another three, with a squadron of Meteors borrowed from the Second Tactical Air Force, to patrol between the guns and London. At night two squadrons of Mosquitos would patrol over the sea and a squadron of Tempests behind the guns. A direct link with radar stations in Belgium would help to give notice of the passage of flying bombs across the northern front of the Allied armies.

One reason why the new sites were not attacked in February was that the enemy was not expected to be in a position to mount a serious offensive for at least some weeks. Nevertheless the opening of attacks from a new area on March 3 found the defences so well prepared that they shot down six of the seven bombs which approached the country in the early hours of the day, missing only the first of all, which fell at Bermondsey just after 3 a.m. A second bout of launchings brought ten bombs within reach of the defences between the afternoon of the same day and noon on March 4. Four were destroyed and two reached Greater London.

By March 6 nine of the twelve batteries ordered south on February 27 had completed the move, and the guns already in position so obviously had the situation well in hand that only one of the remaining three was called upon. For the same reason only two of the ten fighter squadrons which Hill had expected to use were needed. Spitfire fighter-bombers of Fighter Command attacked the Ypenburg site on March 20 and again on March 23, Typhoon fighter-bombers of the Second Tactical Air Force the Vlaardingen site on the second of those days.

After a lull which ended towards midday on March 5, launchings continued intermittently until almost the end of the month. Greater London had its last flying bombs on March 28, when two fell at Chislehurst and Waltham Cross. Thereafter twenty-one bombs approached the country. All succumbed to the defences except one which fell at Datchworth, a village near Hatfield, a few minutes before 9 a.m. on March 29. About an hour later a bomb brought down by the guns came to earth at Iwade, near Sittingbourne. The last bomb of all was shot down by gunners in the 'Strip' at 12.43 p.m. on the same day and fell in the sea off Orfordness. Since March 3, 275 flying bombs had been launched from the three Dutch ramps aligned on London, but only 125 had flown far and straight enough to present a target to the defences. Of thirty-four which guns and fighters failed to destroy, only thirteen reached the target.

Meanwhile Hill's fighter-bombers continued their attacks on targets at and near The Hague, flying more sorties in March than in the previous four months put together, and dropping some six hundred tons of bombs. On March 7 the rocket-troops reported their losses since air attacks began as 51 dead, 117 wounded, and 48 rockets and 69 vehicles damaged. This was not known at the time to Hill or the Air Ministry, but there were indications by the middle of the month that the troops had abandoned not only the Haagsche Bosch and Duindigt but also other positions in that part of The Hague. Thereafter a scarcity of good targets forced the fighter-bombers to devote a good deal of their effort to attacks on communications.

Perhaps partly as a result of the bombing, the scale of attack decreased slightly, and the Germans showed a tendency to bring up supplies under cover of darkness and make an increasing proportion of their launchings in the early morning. Even so, the number of rockets which reached London during the month was only two less than in February, and casualties were fairly heavy, largely because a number of rockets fell in crowded places. On March 8, for example, 233 people were killed or seriously injured by a rocket which struck Smithfield Market in the middle of a busy morning, and on March 27 a block of flats at Stepney was hit early in the day when most of the occupants were at home, with the result that 134 people lost their lives and another 49 were badly hurt. Incidents involving serious loss of life occurred also at Heston, Enfield, West Ham, Deptford, Poplar and Leyton.

It was against this background that the Chiefs of Staff gave final consideration to a proposal from General Pile that he should use some of his anti-aircraft guns to put a curtain of shell-fragments in the radar-predicted path of approaching rockets with the object of exploding them in the air. When the scheme was considered by the War Cabinet 'Crossbow' Committee in January, after Hill had referred it to the Air Ministry as one which contained 'the germ of successful counter-measures', estimates of the odds against success ranged from the hundred to one of Professor Ellis to the thousand to one of Sir Robert Watson Watt. On March 26 a panel of scientists reported that the odds might be as low as thirty to one if four hundred rounds were fired at a given rocket. The Chiefs of Staff, however, were reluctant to risk alarming the public by an unexplained volume of fire, and were therefore not in favour of trying the experiment.

In any case, by the time they announced their decision on March 30, the chance had gone. At 4.45 p.m. on March 27, just under nine and a half hours after the disaster at Stepney, the last long-range rocket to reach the country fell at Orpington in Kent. Since September the launching-troops in Holland had aimed 1,403 rockets at the United Kingdom, all but forty-four of them at London. Of that total, 517 had fallen in the London Civil Defence Region, 537 elsewhere on land, and 61 off-shore but close enough to the coast for their arrival to be noticed. The remaining 288 were wild or abortive shots.

With no more rockets reaching the country after March 27, and no more flying bombs after March 29, Hill ordered that attacks on V.1 and V.2 sites in Holland should cease on April 3. He continued armed reconnaissance sorties as a precautionary measure until April 25. On April 13 radar stations discontinued their special watch for ascending rockets. With the Third Reich on its last legs, the Chiefs of Staff agreed on May 2 to suspend all counter-measures in the light of a report from the Joint Intelligence Committee that there was no risk of further attacks with flying bombs and that the menace of the long-range rocket had assumed minute proportions.

After launching their last rocket on March 27, the troops at

The Hague withdrew in good order to Germany, chiefly because the German High Command believed that their positions were about to be overrun and that they and their equipment might fall intact into Allied hands. On May 9 the bulk of them, with most of the rest of the rocket-launching organisation, surrendered to the United States Ninth Army. So ended a bid which seemed to establish Nazi supremacy in the race for novel means of indiscriminate destruction until the Allies capped it a few months later at Hiroshima and Nagasaki.

11

Inquest

THE V-weapon campaign left a legacy of questions, not all of them susceptible of clear-cut answers. In this chapter an attempt will be made to present some of those questions in the perspective of the years that have elapsed since the last V-weapon fell on British soil.

1. *Was either V.1 or V.2 a new departure in the sense that it introduced a new principle of strategy?*

Pilotless winged missiles and long-range rockets are bombardment weapons, or, in short, artillery. Whether a mere extension of the range of artillery can ever be said to introduce a new principle of strategy can only be a matter of opinion. V.1 and V.2 did not, however, extend the range beyond that already attainable with the manned bomber, itself a form of artillery although often an uncertain and uneconomic one.

2. *Were V.1 and V.2 sound weapons in the military sense?*

A bombardment weapon can be considered sound if it is accurate enough to hit the target, powerful enough to destroy the target or at least damage it severely, and not so vulnerable to counter-bombardment that it is likely to be knocked out before it has earned its keep.

Until comparatively recent years both V.1 and V.2 would probably have been considered thoroughly unsatisfactory on the first ground. V.1 was inherently inaccurate, V.2 not accurate enough, at the stage reached in 1944, to hit a target as large as Norwich once in forty-three rounds, even when fired by a crack unit. Since the introduction of the manned bomber, however, the tendency of practising strategists has been to choose the target to fit the weapon rather than the weapon to fit the target, so that almost any degree of inaccuracy becomes acceptable if the definition of a suitable target can be stretched far enough. By the standards of their day, therefore, both weapons could be reckoned satisfactory from that point of view.

Neither V.1 nor V.2 lacked destructive power, and neither was prohibitively susceptible to counter-bombardment so far as the installations required to launch the missile were concerned. The 'modified' sites for the flying bomb, for example, were not knocked out by attacks made on them after launching began, and there is no convincing evidence that a V.2 launching-platform ever received a direct hit. On the other hand, a useful rate of fire with the flying bomb could be maintained only by the accumulation of large stocks of missiles in underground stores whose exits and entrances did prove vulnerable. Much the same might have proved true of the long-range rocket if the rate of fire attempted had ever reached comparable proportions.

3. *Were the German High Command right, from the German point of view, when they decided to produce the V-weapons, and afterwards to use them?*

Some critics of Hitler's strategy have argued that the productive effort which went into the V-weapons would have been better devoted to the manufacture of substantial numbers of fighters or bombers. Whether that is so depends partly on whether the Germans could have found enough trained crews and enough fuel for a greatly-expanded air force. That question in turn raises so many hypothetical issues that no one in Germany seems to have been able to say where the truth really lay.

Whether the V.1 and V.2 offensives achieved anything of value is an equally controversial question. They brought Germany no direct strategic gain in the shape of positions won or armies or fleets defeated. On the other hand, they and the threat of them caused the Allies to expend on 'secret weapon' targets about 120,000 tons of bombs which they might otherwise have dropped on Germany or used to expedite their victory over German armies in the field. Perhaps the only satisfactory answer to these questions is that Hitler lost the war and committed suicide.

4. *Were V.1 and V.2 'legitimate' weapons from the humanitarian point of view?*

Until fairly recent times the intentional bombardment of non-combatants, except after offers of removal to a place of safety had been refused on their behalf, was generally regarded by soldiers as wrong, although that does not mean that it was never done. Similarly, the sinking of merchant ships with passengers and crews aboard was considered a crime until Germany set a new example with her submarine campaign in the First World War. The underlying principle in both cases was that non-combatants were entitled to sanctuary.

Insofar as the principle of sanctuary may be thought to have been still valid on the outbreak of the Second World War, the British government openly abandoned it in the autumn of 1940 when they planned 'area attacks' on German cities, while the Germans admitted to doing so only when Hitler ordered 'terror attacks of a retaliatory nature' in the spring of 1942. In practice, however, both sides threw their scruples overboard at the moment when they first sent bombers to attack 'military targets' under cover of darkness, knowing that bombs which fell wide were likely to kill non-combatants. The argument that there were no non-combatants in modern war was clearly sophistical, since no definition could make combatants of children in arms and the infirm.

Because of their inaccuracy, both V.1 and V.2 were weapons of indiscriminate destruction. So also was the night bomber as used, for example, by the Germans in the 'Blitz', and by the British in raids on Berlin, Essen, Munich, Hamburg and Cologne in November, 1940, as well as earlier and later.

The answer to the question would seem to be, therefore, that V.1 and V.2 were not legitimate weapons by the standards to which all civilised nations paid at least lip-service until 1915 or later, but were legitimate weapons by those accepted by both sides during the greater part of the Second World War.

5. *Was the Allied search for the V-weapons efficiently conducted?*

The British government were informed in November, 1939, that the Germans were developing large rockets for military purposes and that they had an important experimental station at Peenemünde.

In May, 1942, a British reconnaissance pilot photographed Peenemünde more or less at random. In June of the same year trial launchings of the A-4 rocket began there, and in October the Germans made their first completely successful launching. Towards the end of the year a new source transmitted to London the first of three reports which together indicated that trials of a long-range rocket had been held recently in the neighbourhood.

In spite of the delay in following up the information obtained in 1939, the British authorities thus lost the little time before getting on the trail of the A-4 rocket, as distinct from earlier rockets which were purely experimental and had no direct military value.

In the early part of 1943 the search was pursued with such energy that by April the intelligence staffs were in possession of further reports which linked the trials more precisely with Peenemünde, and of three more sets of photographs.

At that stage, however, the rocket threatened to become a bone of contention between the War Office and the Air Ministry, and for some months the intelligence staffs worked under an independent investigator-in-chief connected with the Ministry of Supply. During and after that time study of the factual evidence was copiously supplemented by speculation on the part of scientific advisers imperfectly acquainted with the latest trends in long-range rocketry, but there is no evidence that progress was slowed down in consequence, although there is evidence that time was wasted on unprofitable lines of enquiry. In the end a good working knowledge of the rocket was obtained before it went into service; meanwhile enough was discovered to justify the deployment of radar, sound-ranging and flash-spotting equipment to keep watch for ascending missiles.

As regards V.1, the decision to develop and produce the weapon was taken on June 19, 1942, and the first practical trials were made in the following December. V.1 was confused by many informants with V.2, but by May, 1943, Mr Duncan Sandys, at that time responsible for investigating the rocket, was aware that pilotless aircraft as well as rockets might be in the offing. By the end of August, nearly ten months before the V.1 offensive began, the intelligence staffs knew that the flying bomb was just as real a threat as the rocket. They also knew the designation of the regiment which was to launch the missiles and the name of its commander. By the end of November they had located ninety-five of the ninety-six launching-sites constructed up to that time, so that they were able to issue target-data in time for attacks on the sites to begin five days later.

6. *Did the Americans give the British their first warning about Peenemünde?*

The British knew about Peenemünde in November, 1939. However, Allen Dulles, at the relevant time senior representative in Switzerland of the United States Office of Strategic Service and afterwards Director of the Central Intelligence Agency, is credited in some quarters with giving them their first hint that the A-4 rocket was being tested there.

This could mean that Dulles handled the agents who told the British late in 1942 and early in 1943 that rocket trials had been held recently at or near Peenemünde, or even that he was himself the 'agent whose reliability was still untested' referred to in the British official history. But it seems very unlikely that he did or was. If anything is certain about Allen Dulles it is that he was a loyal American citizen who would not let material which he was handling go to a foreign government before it reached his own. According to an official citation, he sent his first reports about Peenemünde to his superiors in May, 1943. The British received the crucial information between April and the previous December.

7. Was Bomber Command's raid on Peenemünde worth the loss of forty aircraft?

The number of aircraft which failed to return was just under seven per cent. of the number sent, a serious but not prohibitive rate of loss.

The raid did heavy damage to offices and living-quarters and killed two scientific officers who held key positions, as well as about 750 other people. It was a striking demonstration of the extravagance of bombing, for many of those killed were impressed foreign workers whose deaths were of no benefit to the Allies and were, indeed, regretted by the organisers of the raid.

After the raid the Germans abandoned a plan to assemble production models of the rocket at Peenemünde, Friedrichshafen and Wiener Neustadt, and elected to do all assembly in an underground factory in the Harz Mountains. They also decided to carry out trials with live war-heads at Blizna, in Poland.

The orthodox view is that these moves must have delayed the introduction of the rocket to active service, and that therefore the raid was of great value to the Allies. On the other hand, sceptics point out that the production programme abandoned after the raid was manifestly unsatisfactory. They assert that the Germans would have had to abandon it in any case, and that the raid did them a good turn by putting them in the right frame of mind to make the change without delay. The sceptical also point out that at least one factor which held up production was the discovery at Blizna that fewer than half the launchings attempted were successful, and that most of the rockets successfully launched disintegrated before they reached the target. Had the second of these faults not been discovered before production had gone too far, the V.2 offensive would have been a fiasco.

Whether the Germans would have transferred part of their activities to some place other than Peenemünde if there had been no raid is not known. The presumption is that they would, since they would hardly have wished to launch rockets with live war-heads over German territory, and trials over land were necessary to test the behaviour of the rocket on and shortly before impact. If, however, it were possible to believe that they did not at first mean to make such tests and that only the bombing of Peenemünde led them to do so by enforcing the move to Blizna, then admittedly it would follow that the raid saved them from making themselves a laughing-stock by going into action with an imperfect weapon. The only evidence which points in that direction is that they did, in fact, begin production before full reports of the tests at Blizna became available, and had to interrupt it when they found that modification of the design was necesssary to avoid premature disintegration.

8. *Apart from the raid on Peenemünde, did the Allies make good use of their information when planning and executing offensive counter-measures before the first of the V-weapons went into service?*

Beginning in August, 1943, the Allies made heavy attacks on the 'large sites' at Watten and elsewhere in Northern France. Clearly these attacks were justified, even though the Allies did not know the purpose of the sites. The Germans would hardly build such massive constructions merely as a hoax.

The three thousand tons of bombs which the Allies aimed at ski sites in December, 1943, were also well spent. The effect was virtually to knock out the sites, for the attacks strengthened General Heinemann's distrust of them and thus contributed to his decision to abandon them.

A similar weight of bombs aimed at the 'modified' sites as soon as their construction began might have had a profound effect. The German High Command might even have concluded that they had no hope of mounting a successful V.1 offensive. As it was, German security and counter-espionage prevented the Allies from informing themselves about the 'modified' sites until the psychological moment was past. Even then they waited until the new sites were in use before attacking them. Whether this was a blunder, or alternatively a wise decision in view of the difficulty of knocking out the sites, is an open question.

Between January and mid-June, 1944, the Allies aimed a further twenty thousand tons of bombs at the ski sites. If this was an over-insurance against the risk that the ski sites might still be used, it was partly justified by the fact that the first 'modified' site was not located by photographic reconnaissance until late in April. After the middle of May, however, by which time twenty 'modified' sites had been located, it was a fair inference that the new sites were meant to replace the ski sites and that the Germans were not likely to use both. For reasons which are understandable but hard to elucidate without close argument, the Air Ministry and the Allied Air Commander none the less continued, even after that date, to act on the assumption that the few ski sites which they believed to be still intact were a more immediate danger than the unbombed 'modified' sites.

9. *If the ski sites had not been bombed, would the V.1 offensive have started before D-day instead of after it?*

Series production of V.1 began late in September, 1943, less than three months before the date first fixed for the opening of the offensive. When it became clear that the date could not be met, General Heinemann was asked whether he could start in January. He replied that possibly the weapon might be ready in May or June. His forecast may have been coloured by his poor opinion of the ski sites, but the implication seems to have been that the governing factor was the state of readiness of the missile itself, not that of the sites.

Thus the evidence would seem to justify the assumption that the offensive *might* have started before D-day if the ski sites had not been bombed, but not the assumption that it necessarily *would* have done so. The difficulties of supply which dogged Colonel Wachtel when he tried to start his offensive on June 12 might have been present in even greater force if he had tried to start a month earlier.

10. *Did the bombing of the ski sites prevent the Germans from launching thousands of flying bombs a day, instead of the hundred or so a day which they did launch?*

There is no evidence, and no reason to suppose, that the ski sites would have been capable of a substantially greater rate of fire than the 'modified' sites. Irrespective of the sites used, the scale of attack could not have exceeded that of which sixteen launching-batteries manning sixty-four positions were capable. Nor could it have exceeded, except for brief periods, the rate at which stocks of missiles and fuel could be replenished. Had the Germans used the ski sites instead of the 'modified' sites, they might have been able to keep more missiles immediately at hand, but that would not necessarily have increased their rate of fire. At 10 p.m. on June 15, 1944, Wachtel had well over eight hundred missiles at his sites. Yet his effort during the next fourteen hours was only 244 missiles from 55 sites aligned on London and about 50 from a small number of sites aligned on Southampton. Clearly the number of missiles at the sites was not the decisive factor.

11. *Could the Germans have used V.2 before D-day if, in August, 1943, the Allies had not bombed Peenemünde and begun to bomb the 'large sites'?*

The bombing of the 'large sites' had no significant effect on the date of the V.2 offensive; the effects of the raid on Peenemünde have been discussed under Question 7.

It is extremely improbable that V.2 could have been ready by or before D-day in any circumstances. Originally the Germans hoped to use both V.1 and V.2 in December, 1943. When Heinemann reported that V.1 would not be ready before May or June, he added that V.2 would not be ready until much later. In April, 1944, General Metz, who then commanded the launching-troops, stated that the rocket was not yet fit for use in war and that recruitment and training were unsatisfactory. Next month he and General Dornberger, who was responsible for training and also for technical development, agreed that the weapon might be ready about the beginning of September.

12. *Did the Allies make good use of their bomber forces to counter the V.1 offensive once it began?*

Chiefly, it would seem, because the Allies failed to hit upon a person or agency able to draw up simple target-lists to which all operational commanders could agree and by which all would abide, their use of their air striking power to counter the V.1 offensive was illogical and extravagant to an almost incredible degree. About 74,000 tons of bombs were devoted to offensive counter-measures between June 13 and September 1, 1944. A great part of this huge tonnage was aimed at targets of doubtful relevance or of no relevance at all. These included ski sites and 'supply sites' long since abandoned by the enemy; 'large sites' of which it could safely be said that, no matter how important they might be in the abstract, they were not being used for launching flying bombs; production centres whose connection with the missile was tenuous or purely conjectural; and even power stations.

By the end of the third week in June the keys to the V.1 supply system were known to be three underground stores in the valley of the Oise and Champagne. A number of attacks were made on these stores; for ten days immediately after one of them the number of missiles reaching the United Kingdom fell by nearly a third. The stores could not be bombed out of existence, but this experience suggested that the Allies could not do better than devote their entire effort for at least some weeks to a resolute attempt to isolate them and keep them isolated. Yet, instead of doing so, they continued to rain bombs on such objectives as production centres, whose destruction could not conceivably affect the rate of fire for many weeks, even if they had any connection with V.1 at all. A list issued for the guidance of operational commanders in the middle of August contained 122 targets arranged in seven priorities and ten sub-categories. Its successor raised the number of targets to 130 and the number of sub-categories to fourteen.

13. *Did the air defences really get the better of the flying bomb in August, or did the number of missiles reaching London tail off merely because the Germans began to withdraw their launching-troops in face of the Allied advance?*

Colonel Wachtel did begin to thin out his line about the middle of August, but the troops which remained were still capable of launching a hundred or more missiles a day right up to the last few days of the month. On August 28, for example, 97 missiles, exclusive of grossly defective shots which usually accounted for about one-fifth of all launchings, approached the United Kingdom; the defences brought down 90, and only four reached London. During the last seven weeks of the offensive from ramps in Northern France, the defences destroyed an average of 44 missiles a day out of 87 launched and 76 which approached the country, and during the last three weeks only one missile out of every seven launched reached London. These and other statistics based on a comparison of British and German records make it clear that the defences did gain the upper hand, and that the decline in the number of missiles reaching London was not due merely to a lower scale of attack.

14. *Why did the German High Command allow a heavily-censored Press to announce that the Allies had found a counter-measure to V.1?*

Presumably to take some of the sting out of the loss of the launching-areas in Northern France, perhaps also to prepare the minds of the newspaper-reading public for the idea that V.2 was an improvement on V.1, not a mere supplement or stop-gap.

15. *Did the Allies find a counter-measure to V.2?*

No. Armed reconnaissance and fighter-bomber attacks were only palliatives, although the latter achieved some good results.

Air Marshal Hill believed, however, that there were two *potential* counter-measures.

In the first place, he was impressed by the success of some of the attacks made on underground V.1 stores in France. Such meagre rocket-stores as existed at The Hague were not attractive targets for heavy and medium bombers; hence Air Chief Marshal Harris and Air Marshal Coningham did not respond very eagerly to suggestions that they should be bombed. Hill was convinced, however, that the Germans would not be able to increase their scale of attack to any great extent without building up substantial supplies in the forward area. In that case worth-while targets would present themselves, and bombing might provide the answer.

Secondly, he had faith in General Pile's plan to blow up approaching rockets by putting a curtain of shell-fragments in their path. When the Chiefs of Staff turned down Pile's proposals three months after Hill first asked the Air Ministry to consider it, they forfeited a unique chance of gaining valuable experience of a new technique at a trifling cost. Even if no hits were scored, Britain would have won the moral advantage of being the first nation to experiment with anti-missile missiles in realistic conditions.

16. *What light did the V-weapons seem to throw on the development of future weapon-systems?*

V.1, flying straight and level, was easily brought down by guns and fighters. The missile would present a more difficult target to the defences if it were made to change course during flight by radio-control, but interference with the control-system would then offer the defenders an alternative means of making the weapon ineffective. On the assumption that successors to V.1 were likely to be as vulnerable to the defensive methods of their day as V.1 was to the guns and fighters of 1944, there seemed to be little or no future for pilotless winged missiles as long-range bombardment weapons.

V.2, on the other hand, was obviously capable of far-reaching development. German technicians were already groping towards an inter-continental rocket capable of crossing the Atlantic. Hence the general expectation at the end of the

Second World War was that long-range and very-long-range ballistic missiles, some with nuclear war-heads and some without, would replace manned bombers for many purposes within ten years or so.

On the defensive side, anti-aircraft guns using modern predictors and firing shells with proximity-fuses proved capable towards the end of the V.1 offensive of destroying up to eighty per cent. of the targets presented to them. Homing devices might be expected to make defensive projectiles highly effective even against targets which could dodge. Thus the future seemed to lie with anti-aircraft and anti-missile missiles rather than defensive fighters.

Britain, with her wartime experience of V-weapons and an air defence system vastly superior at every stage of the war to all comparable systems elsewhere in the world, seemed likely to become a vigorous competitor in the missile race, especially on the defensive side. Sir Roderic Hill's appointment to the new post of Air Member for Technical Services in the Air Ministry at the end of the war in Europe could be taken as a small but possibly significant pointer in that direction, especially as he was a promising candidate for the key-position of Chief of the Air Staff in succession to Air Chief Marshal Tedder.

In the outcome, scarcely any of these expectations was fulfilled. Pilotless aircraft on the lines of V.1 were not dropped. Long-range ballistic missiles did not supersede the manned bomber within ten years or anything like that time. Anti-aircraft missiles did not so much replace fighters as compete with them, and anti-missile missiles threatened to be so difficult and expensive to produce that even the richest and most technically advanced nations fought shy of them. Britain did not take a leading part in the missile race. Hill did not become Chief of the Air Staff but left the Air Ministry and took up the task of helping to double Britain's output of technicians.

So far as the West was concerned, the race to be first with the inter-continental ballistic missile and the anti-missile missile was thus left to the United States. American strategists, however, elected to pursue a number of competing aims, with the inevitable result. Navaho, an ambitious offspring of V.1 with ram-jet propulsion and a reputed range of 5,000 miles, cost seven hundred million dollars before it was consigned to the limbo of best-forgotten things.* Millions were spent on manned bomber programmes which led nowhere. To produce and use a satisfactory inter-continental ballistic missile was said to be impossible without data unobtainable except with the aid of a satellite which the Americans did not have.

Thus the decade of progress expected to follow the conclusion of hostilities in Europe proved, from the strategic point of view, a decade of progress only for the Russians. The huge lead in the field of military technology which the West could claim over the East when Kammler's troops surrendered in 1945 was whittled away until, by 1957, the East seemed not merely to have drawn level, but even to have drawn ahead. Yet all this could have been avoided if, from the moment when the descent of the first V.2 on British soil marked the dawn of a new age, the West had observed the age-old principle of economy of effort and concentration on the aim.

---

* Lieutenant-General James M. Gavin, *War and Peace in the Space Age* (1959), p. 30. General Gavin was Chief of Research and Development in the United States Army until he retired to write his book.

Chronological Summary

1907
Victor de Karavodine granted French patent for pulse-jet using low-pressure blower and sparking-plug.

1910
Georges Marconnet, Belgian engineer, granted French patent for pulse-jet suitable for aircraft.

1919
René Lorin, French artillery officer, publishes proposals for bombardment of distant objectives with remotely-controlled pilotless aircraft, propelled by pulse-jet or ram-jet. Claims to have studied subject since 1907.
Robert H. Goddard, American inventor, proposes gaseous fuels for high-altitude rockets.

1923
Herman Oberth, Transylvanian Saxon, proposes liquid-fuelled rockets for interplanetary flight.

1926

Goddard launches rocket propelled by petrol (gasoline) and liquid oxygen.

1929

Oberth embodies proposals in book which comes to notice of highly-placed German officers.

1930

Paul Schmidt, German inventor, designs pulse-jet afterwards developed as Schmidt duct.

1931

Walter Dornberger, German artillery officer with technical background, joins Ballistics and Munitions Section of Ordnance Branch under War Office. Begins to develop solid-fuelled rockets on lines foreshadowed by Swedish ballistics expert Unge, and liquid-fuelled rockets on lines proposed by Oberth and others.

1932

Dornberger sets team headed by Wernher von Braun to work on 'liquid' rockets.

1934

Schmidt proposes 'flying torpedo' powered by Schmidt duct.

About same time, or perhaps later, Argus Motorenwerke, German aero-engine firm, also become interested in pulse-jet systems. Ultimately design-staff headed by Fritz Gosslau develop Argus duct independently of Schmidt.

Dornberger's team launch two liquid-propelled rockets, with gyroscopic stabilisation, from island of Borkum.

1936
Encouraged by General von Fritsch, Commander-in-Chief of German Army, Dornberger plans large rocket on lines of subsequent A-4 (V.2).
German War Office and Air Ministry agree to share cost of developing site at Peenemünde for Army and Luftwaffe experimental stations.
Goddard publishes paper on liquid propulsion for rockets.

1937
Dornberger's team launch two rockets of A-3 series from Greifswalder Oie.

1939

Spring   Hitler sees combustion-test of propulsion-unit for large rockets at Kummersdorf, and is not impressed.

July   German pilotless aircraft, powered by piston-engine and intended for reconnaissance of Maginot Line, demonstrated at Rechlin.

Late Summer   German Air Ministry invite Argus Motorenwerke to submit proposals for pilotless missile with range of 350 miles. Argus propose remotely-controlled missile propelled by piston-engine, turbo-jet or ducted fan.

Early November   British government receive anonymous Oslo Report on German technical develop-

	ments. Large rockets and Peenemünde both mentioned.
November 13	Argus hold trial of Argus duct.
November 30	Argus duct demonstrated to Air Ministry. Schmidt duct demonstrated at or about same time.

1942

Spring	Argus advised by German Air Ministry not to drop pilotless-aircraft project.
March 28	British Bomber Command try out new fire-raising technique at Lübeck. More than 200 acres of buildings destroyed.
April 14	Hitler orders 'terror attacks of a retaliatory nature'.
May 15	Chance cover of Peenemünde by British reconnaissance aircraft reveals unexplained constructions.
Early June	Trial launchings of A-4 rocket begin at Peenemünde.
June 19	Dr Gosslau of Argus gives Field-Marshal Milch of German Air Ministry oral description, and makes rough drawing, of proposed bombardment missile with wings and pulse-jet propulsion. Milch orders development on highest priority by Fieseler, Argus and Askania jointly, with Staff-Engineer Brée as co-ordinator for Air Ministry.
October 3	A-4 rocket launched at Peenemünde reaches height of 50 miles, attains speed of 3,300 m.p.h., and travels 120 miles along predicted line of shoot.
Early December	Unpowered prototype of missile described June 19 launched from aircraft at Peene-

	münde. Missile first called Fieseler 103, afterwards FZG. 76 (V.1).
December 24	First trial launching of Fieseler 103 from ramp, also at Peenemünde.
Towards end of year	Allied agent of unknown reliability sends first of three reports pointing to recent trials of large rockets near Swinemünde.

1943

Early in year	Further reports from Allied agents link trials of large rockets with Peenemünde. Evidence from prisoners of war tends to confirm existence of weapon.
Early March	Hitler dreams that A-4 rocket will never be used against England.
Early April	Review of air photographs of Peenemünde confirms presence of several unexplained structures, including large elliptical earthwork.
April 11	Vice-Chief of Imperial General Staff circulates paper on German long-range rocket development; adds speculative account of weapon.
mid-April	Mr Duncan Sandys of Ministry of Supply appointed to investigate threat from large rocket and suggest counter-measures.
	Air Ministry order photographic interpreters to give high priority to 'secret weapons' investigation.
May 9	Mr Sandys asks photographic interpreters orally for news of pilotless aircraft as well as large rockets.
May 14	Sandys makes first interim report. Suggests

tentatively that rocket may weigh seventy tons and have ten-ton war-head.

June 2	Air photographs of Peenemünde show columnar object about forty feet high on foreshore.
June 23	Air photographs of Peenemünde show finned objects about forty feet long lying horizontally on vehicles within elliptical earthwork.
Before June 28	Well-placed informant tells British authorities that secret weapon to be used against London is air-mine with wings, long-distance steering and rocket-drive, and is launched by catapult.
June 28	Third interim report from Mr Sandys puts weight of rocket at possibly sixty to a hundred tons, including two to eight tons of explosive.
June 29	Defence Committee (Operations) consider third interim report. Lord Cherwell thinks rocket must be hoax. Dr R. V. Jones of Air Intelligence stresses value of Peenemünde to Germans. Committee sanction bombing of Peenemünde. Sandys and Jones to look into 'air-mine with wings'.
July	Hitler sees film of launching of A-4 in October, 1942. Apologises for previous scepticism and decrees highest priority throughout industry and armed forces. About same time, Long Range Bombardment Commission recommend development of both A-4 and FZG. 76.
August 12	Allied agent names A-4 as weapon distinct from winged missile.

August 17	British Bomber Command attack Peenemünde. Plan to assemble rockets there and at two other places afterwards abandoned in favour of assembly at Niedersachswerfen. Most trial launchings transferred to Blizna.
August 27	United States bombers attack mysterious 'large site' at Watten.
August 30	New source informs British authorities that Flakregiment 155 (W), commanded by Colonel Wachtel, will be deployed in France about beginning of November and will man 108 catapults. Confuses FZG. 76 with A-4. Shortly afterwards brief particulars received of pilotless aircraft down on Bornholm.
Late summer	Mr I. Lubbock, British petroleum expert, gains knowledge of experiments with liquid fuels in United States.
Beginning of September	Dornberger appointed Special Commissioner (Army); also ARKO (later HARKO) 91.
Early September	Air Ministry assume responsibility for investigation of German pilotless aircraft and jet propulsion in place of Mr Sandys.
September 7	United States bombers make further attack on Watten.
Late September	Series production of FZG. 76 begins at Fallersleben.
October	One company of Germans signals regiment specialising in radio-beams and radar known to Air Ministry to be deployed in Pomerania and on Rügen and Bornholm. Evidence received that company is tracking pilotless aircraft launched from Peenemünde and

	from neighbourhood. Air Ministry ask for reconnaissance of Zinnowitz to confirm presence of appropriate equipment.
October 21	Sandys asks for fresh reconnaissance of Northern France.
Late October	Part of Flakregiment 155 (W) leaves Zinnowitz for Northern France.
	French source describes eight mysterious sites under construction in Northern France.
November 3	Sites described by French source photographed from air. Ski-shaped buildings and other characteristic features common to all. More ski sites soon discovered.
November 8-10	Sir Stafford Cripps holds special enquiry at request of Prime Minister. Air Ministry report nineteen sites found up to midnight November 7, twenty-six by November 10. Cripps concludes seventy-ton rocket with ten-ton war-head not impossible, pilotless aircraft more urgent threat.
November 13	Section Officer Babington Smith of Central Interpretation Unit finds unidentified midget aircraft on photographs of Peenemünde taken June 23.
November 18	Air Ministry assume responsibility for investigating rocket in place of Mr Sandys.
November 28	Unable to photograph Berlin because of cloud, Squadron Leader Merifield of Photographic Reconnaissance Unit covers Peenemünde and Zinnowitz.
Last week in November	Number of ski sites seen on air photographs rises to ninety-five.
December 1	Section Officer Babington Smith sees ramp on old cover of Peenemünde. Later in day,

	sees Merifield's recent cover and finds midget aircraft on same ramp. Merifield's cover of Zinnowitz shows ramp on foundations similar to those at ski sites.
Early December	Flakregiment 155 (W) and HARKO 91 placed under command of newly-formed LXV Armee Korps (Lieutenant-General Erich Heinemann). Major-General Richard Metz succeeds Dornberger as HARKO 91.
Early December	Air Marshal R. M. (later Sir Roderic) Hill, commanding Air Defence of Great Britain, ordered to prepare plan of defence against pilotless aircraft.
December 5	Allied aircraft begin to attack ski sites.
December	Heinemann tours ski sites and finds them insecure, conspicuous, needlessly elaborate and highly vulnerable. Reports that FZG. 76, but not A-4, may be ready by May or June.

1944

January 2	Hill submits plan for defence of London, Bristol and Solent against pilotless aircraft. 1,332 guns to be deployed.
Early January	Flakregiment 155 (W) abandon ski sites, except as blind, in favour of 'modified' sites. Eight supply sites in Northern France abandoned in favour of underground stores in valley of Oise and Champagne. Security and counter-espionage tightened.
January	Series production of A-4 begins at Niedersachswerfen. Soon interrupted to allow modification of design.
Early February	Hill ordered to recast plan in interests of

L

	invasion forces. Reduces allotment of guns to 570 until D-day, 384 thereafter.
February	Existence of 'modified' sites first reported to British authorities.
March	Reports of German activities at Blizna reach London from Polish sources.
after mid-March	German authorities at Blizna report 57 attempted launchings up to middle of month, only 26 successful. All but four of rockets successfully launched disintegrated before reaching target.
end March	A-4 launching-troops about one-quarter ready.
April	Metz reports A-4 not yet fit for use in war, recruitment and training unsatisfactory.
April 27	Allied photographic interpreters identify 'modified' site at Belhamelin. First of twenty found up to mid-May.
May	A-4 demonstrated at Blizna. Metz, Dornberger and others agree weapon may be fit for use about beginning of September. Launchings contemplated from 45 groups of platforms and two 'large sites' in Northern France.
May 27	Allied fighter-bombers make experimental attack on 'modified' site. No further attacks on such sites before opening of V.1 offensive or for some time after.
June 6	D-day. Allies land in Western Normandy. Heinemann orders Wachtel to prepare for immediate V.1 offensive.
June 10	Air Staff predict that 'modified' sites will not be ready for use on any appreciable scale for some weeks.

June 10: late afternoon	Belgian informant reports that train carrying 99 rocket-like objects towards French frontier has passed through Ghent.
June 11	Allies make first photographic reconnaissance of 'modified' sites since June 4. Rails on launching-ramps at four of nine sites photographed, characteristic square building completed at six.
June 11	Summoned to Heinemann's headquarters, Wachtel agrees to start offensive next day, but stresses difficulties.
June 12: morning	Air Staff warn Chiefs of Staff and others of activity at 'modified' sites.
June 12: evening	70 to 80 'modified' sites north and east of Seine structurally ready, 54 or 55 with launching-rails fitted. 873 missiles at sites, but dummy missiles for practice launchings scarce and safety equipment lacking.
June 12: about 11 p.m.	Wachtel postpones firing of intended salvo from approximately 11.15 p.m. June 12 to approximately 12.15 a.m. June 13.
June 12: 11.50 p.m.	Wachtel orders no salvo before 3.30 a.m. June 13. Sites to fire independently as they become ready.
June 13: 4.18 a.m.	First of four missiles to reach United Kingdom during early hours falls at Swanscombe, Kent. One of ten despatched.
June 13: early morning	LXV Armee Korps order suspension of launchings until further notice.
June 13: morning	Chiefs of Staff endorse Hill's decision not to order planned deployment. Sir Charles Portal, Chief of Air Staff, suggests bombing supply sites. Lord Cherwell sceptical.
June 13: later	War Cabinet agree that Supreme Com-

mander shall be asked to sanction bombing of supply sites.

June 13	A-4 launched from Peenemünde comes down on Swedish soil.
June 13 to June 15	United States bombers attack two supply sites, one several times.
June 15: 10 p.m.	Wachtel launches first of 244 missiles despatched during next 14 hours from 55 'modified' sites aligned on London.
June 16: morning	Chiefs of Staff endorse Hill's decision to order planned deployment. Minister of Home Security tells House of Commons that attacks with pilotless aircraft (afterwards called flying bombs) have begun.
June 16: afternoon	'Staff conference' under Prime Minister authorises Hill to redistribute defences as necessary.
June 16	Bomber Command make night attack on supply sites at request of Air Chief Marshal Leigh-Mallory, Allied Air Commander.
June 17	Bomber Command again make night attack on supply sites.
June 18	Crucial importance of underground stores in valley of Oise and Champagne strongly suspected in London. Air Chief Marshal Harris of Bomber Command unwilling to attack supply sites again without fresh evidence. Harris and his American counterpart, General Doolittle, dissatisfied with attention paid to case for concerted attack on 'modified' sites.
June 18: 11.20 a.m.	Flying bomb hits Royal Military Chapel, Wellington Barracks, killing or seriously

	injuring 189 civilians and members of the fighting services.
June 18	General Eisenhower, Supreme Allied Commander, rules that long-range weapon targets must take precedence over everything except urgent requirements of battle in Normandy.
June 19	Hill gives freedom of action to fighters in good weather, to gunners in bad weather. Special rules for middling weather.
June 20	War Cabinet 'Crossbow' Committee under Duncan Sandys receives watching brief over counter-measures to long-range weapons.
June 20	United States bombers attack Fallersleben.
June 21	All balloons and most guns ordered to move June 16 in position; together bringing down flying bombs at rate of eight to ten a day. Twelve fighter squadrons bringing down thirty a day. About fifty a day reaching Greater London.
June 21 to June 30	Role of underground stores in valley of Oise confirmed. United States bombers attack both.
June 26	Hill issues codified rules for engagement.
June 28	Number of guns deployed on North Downs reaches 785, of which 363 heavy. Static guns on special platforms beginning to replace mobile guns.
July 1	Number of balloons on Cobham-Limpsfield ridge reaches 1,000. 750 more to be added by July 8.
July 4	Bomber Command make night attack on underground store at Saint-Leu-d'Esserent.

July 7	Bomber Command make further night attack on Saint-Leu-d'Esserent.
July 8	American spokesman voices dissatisfaction of British and American bomber commanders with Air Ministry's choice of long-range weapon targets.
July 8 to July 15	Average number of flying bombs approaching United Kingdom falls from 100 to 70 a day. Defences bring down 40 a day; 25 a day reach Greater London.
July 10	Hill decides to banish fighters from gun-belt in all circumstances after middle of month.
About July 11	Lieutenant-General Sir Frederick Pile, commanding Anti-Aircraft Command, suggests removing to gun-belt on North Downs about 600 light guns deployed on South Coast.
July 12	Hill tells Deputy Senior Air Staff Officer, Air Commodore Ambler, to draw up paper explaining why fighters must be banished from gun-belt. Ambler convinced by own reasoning that logical solution is to move gun-belt to South Coast.
July 13	Sir Robert Watson Watt, inventor of radar, confirms Ambler's solution best from radar point of view. General Pile and Air Vice-Marshal Saunders, commanding fighter group concerned, also in favour. Hill orders move without consulting Air Ministry. Tells Leigh-Mallory half-measures worse than useless.
mid-July	First instalment of remains of rocket down in Sweden reaches Royal Aircraft Establishment, Farnborough.

mid-July	Air Ministry admonish Hill for moving guns on own responsibility.
July 16	Dr Jones reports rocket in production; weight of war-head possibly three to seven tons.
July 17	All heavy guns in new positions.
July 17 to July 22	204 flying bombs reach Greater London out of 473 approaching United Kingdom.
July 19: dawn	New gun-belt has 412 heavy guns, 1,184 light guns and 200 rocket-barrels ready for action.
July 20	Attempt to assassinate Hitler fails.
July 21	Anglo-American Joint 'Crossbow' Target Priorities Committee assumes responsibility for listing long-range weapon targets in order of priority.
July 22	Anglo-American Combined Operational Planning Committee undertakes planning of Allied air offensive against long-range weapon targets. Leigh-Mallory still nominally responsible for co-ordination, but no power over heavy bomber forces.
July 24	Mr Sandys suggests that introduction of rocket to active service may be imminent.
July 28	Polish informant from Blizna reaches London after cycling 200 miles through enemy-held territory to embark in Allied aircraft. Confirms A-4 rocket not ready.
Late July	Last instalment of remains of rocket down in Sweden reaches Farnborough after travelling by sea.
Late July	Overall performance of defences against flying bomb begins to show marked upward trend.

July 31	Reconstruction of rocket down in Sweden begins at Farnborough.
July 31	British mission reaches Teheran for purpose of visiting Blizna as soon as situation on Eastern Front and Soviet authorities permit.
End July	Weight of bombs aimed at long-range weapon targets since mid-June reaches nearly 50,000 tons.
August 6	Hitler appoints Heinrich Himmler Special Commissioner for A-4 matters.
August 10	Dr Jones reports that A-4 weighs about twelve tons and has one-ton war-head.
mid-August	Wachtel begins to withdraw troops and equipment from Northern France.
August 27	Jones presents comprehensive report on A-4 in light of reconstruction at Farnborough and material captured in France.
August 28	Defences bring down 90 bombs out of 97 approaching United Kingdom. Four reach Greater London.
August 29	Hitler approves plan for A-4 offensive against London from area Tournai-Ghent.
August 30	Area Antwerp-Malines substituted for area Tournai-Ghent.
August 30	Heinemann relinquishes responsibility for A-4 offensive, nominally to Metz, in effect to Himmler's deputy, SS General Kammler.
August 30	Hill's fighters begin armed reconnaissance of presumed A-4 launching-area in France and Flanders.
End August	Kammler establishes headquarters at Cleve but moves almost immediately to Berg en Del, near Nijmegen.

August 31 to September 1	Bomber Command aim nearly 3,000 tons of bombs at rocket stores in France, no longer in use. Weight of bombs aimed at long-range weapon targets reaches 82,348 tons since mid-June, nearly 118,000 tons since August, 1943.
September 1	Rear party of Flakregiment 155 (W) brings main phase of V.1 offensive to close by firing last round from French soil before moving to Antwerp area and afterwards Deventer. About 9,000 flying bombs (including more than 2,000 abortive or bad shots) aimed at United Kingdom since mid-June.
Early September	Air Ministry send Hill letter of approbation. 2,222 bombs brought down by defences out of 3,791 approaching United Kingdom since guns moved in July. Total since mid-June, 3,563 out of 6,725.
Early September	Leigh-Mallory moves main headquarters to Continent. Nominal responsibility for co-ordinating offensive counter-measures to long-range weapons devolves on Hill.
Early September	British mission reaches Blizna.
September 2	Air Staff predict that threat from A-4 will cease when all Northern France and Belgium within 200 miles of London 'neutralised'.
September 4	Heinemann and staff narrowly escape capture at Waterloo, near Brussels, by moving to Deventer.
September 4	Hill's fighters compelled by Allied advance to discontinue armed reconnaissance of presumed A-4 launching-area. Hill learns

that Chiefs of Staff regard threat to London from A-4 as over, but is warned by own staff that A-4 can still reach London from Western Holland.

September 5 — Air-launching unit working from Dutch bases since July aim nine or more flying bombs at London from east before moving to North-West Germany.

September 5 — Hill learns that review of A-4 situation by Vice-Chiefs has led Chiefs to Staff to conclude that watch for rockets should continue, chiefly as precaution against attacks on targets other than London.

September 6 — Vice-Chiefs of Staff report formally that A-4 attacks on London need no longer be expected; Hill and staff still prepared for attacks beginning first half September.

September 6 — Kammler orders two A-4 launching-batteries (Gruppe Nord) to The Hague for attacks on London; Gruppe Süd (two batteries near Euskirchen, with experimental battery attached) to prepare for attacks on targets in France and Belgium.

September 6 — Experimental battery make two unsuccessful attempts to fire at Paris.

September 8: 8.30 a.m. — Rocket launched by experimental battery falls in built-up area of Paris. Battery afterwards moves to Walcheren to augment attack on London.

September 8: 6.43 p.m. — Rocket launched from The Hague falls at Chiswick, killing or seriously injuring thirteen people. No casualties caused by rocket which falls near Epping sixteen seconds later.

September 9 to September 17	Allied informants send numerous reports of launchings from The Hague and storage at Raaphorst, Eikenhorst and Ter Horst, in suburb of Wassenaar; Walcheren also mentioned. Hill asks Bomber Command to attack Eikenhorst and Ter Horst.
September 14	Before receiving Hill's request, Bomber Command attack Raaphorst.
September 14	Experimental battery begin attacks on London from Walcheren.
September 16	About fifteen aircraft of air-launching unit open new phase of V.1 offensive with attacks on London from north-east.
September 16 to September 19	Hill orders guns to area Clacton-Harwich.
September 17	Bomber Command attack Eikenhorst.
September 17	Allies begin airborne landings Nijmegen-Arnhem. Kammler moves to Darfeld; orders Gruppe Nord and experimental battery to Burgsteinfurt and Zwolle. Allied informants report rocket-troops leaving The Hague.
September 18	Gruppe Nord fire last rocket of first phase of V.2 offensive before completing move. Sixteen rockets in London Civil Defence Region since September 8, eleven elsewhere in Southern England or close off-shore.
September 23 to October 7	Bomber Command and United States Eighth Air Force make several attacks on base of air-launching unit at Handorf-bei-Münster.
Before September 25	Kammler orders experimental battery to Staveren, Friesland, for attacks on Norwich and Ipswich.

171

September 25 — Chiefs of Staff recommend no immediate public announcement about rocket in view of lull.

September 25: 7.10 p.m. — Rocket launched by experimental battery falls at Hoxne, Suffolk, opening new phase of V.2 offensive.

September 30 — Kammler orders one battery of Gruppe Nord back to The Hague for renewed attacks on London.

October 1 — Second Tactical Air Force, headquarters Brussels, assumes responsibility for armed reconnaissance of rocket-launching areas beyond Hill's reach; e.g. Staveren.

October 2 — Chief of Imperial General Staff predicts Antwerp and Brussels may become main V.2 targets.

October 3 — Allied informant reports some rocket-troops may have returned to The Hague.

October 3: late evening — Gruppe Nord open new series of attacks on London. Rocket falls at Leytonstone.

Early October — Leigh-Mallory rules responsibility of Second Tactical Air Force for armed reconnaissance of suspected rocket-sites unaffected by resumption of attacks on London.

October 11 — Organisation set up at Supreme Head-quarters, Versailles, to investigate long-range weapon attacks on Continental targets and co-ordinate counter-measures.

October 12 — Experimental battery ceases fire from Staveren. 43 rockets aimed at Norwich since October 3 and one at Ipswich. No hits on either target.

October 15 — Allied Expeditionary Air Force (Leigh-Mallory) disbanded. Air Defence of Great

Britain (Hill) reverts to old name and status as Fighter Command.

October 16 to October 18 Hill asks Bomber Command and No. 2 Group, Second Tactical Air Force, to attack five selected targets at or near The Hague.

October 17 Air Ministry and Supreme Headquarters sanction geographical division of responsibility for armed reconnaissance between Fighter Command and Second Tactical Air Force. Hill provides nucleus of new organisation created October 11; gives Supreme Commander No. 105 Mobile Air Reporting Unit and 11th Survey Regiment.

October 18 No. 12 Group, Fighter Command, responsible for armed reconnaissance of The Hague.

October 21 Kammler reinforces launching-units at The Hague.

October 24 Hill urges Air Ministry to expedite bombing of aerodromes used by V.1 air-launching unit and of V.2 targets proposed October 16 and 18.

November 1 Two rockets at Camberwell and Deptford kill or seriously injure more than 120 people.

November 8 German authorities announce publicly that V.2 offensive against London has begun.

November 10 British government acknowledge that United Kingdom is under bombardment with rockets, but do not mention London.

mid-November Strength of air-launching unit reaches three Gruppen.

November 17 Hill again urges bombing of proposed V.1 and V.2 targets and asks for greater latitude for his fighter-bombers. Suggests approach to Netherlands government in London.

173

November 21   Netherlands government agree to raise no immediate objection to well-chosen attacks on rocket sites. No promise of direct participation by Bomber Command or Second Tactical Air Force.

November 25   Rocket hits crowded building in New Cross Road, killing or seriously injuring 268 people.

December 20   Hill asks Air Ministry to consider proposal by General Pile to explode anti-aircraft shells in radar-predicted path of oncoming rocket.

December 24   About fifty aircraft aim flying bombs at Manchester. Thirty bombs cross coast, one reaches target. More than a hundred civilian casualties.

December 25   Hill extends special gun defences northwards to Filey.

1945

January 1
to
January 15   Average number of rockets reaching United Kingdom rises to eight a day. Comparative figures four a day mid-December, seven a day late November, three a day September 8 to November 17.

January 14   Last air-launched flying bomb to reach United Kingdom falls at Hornsey. 403 brought down by defences since September 16, 1944, out of 638 approaching United Kingdom and about 1,200 launched.

mid-January   Kammler gains effective control of V.1 as well as V.2.

January 15   War Cabinet 'Crossbow' Committee consider Pile's project. Scientists disagree.

January 22	Second Tactical Air Force attack liquid-oxygen factory at Alblasserdam.
February: third week	Allied informants report much activity in Haagsche Bosch, wooded park where up to twenty to thirty rockets at a time seen on air photographs since December.
February 21 and 22	Hill's fighter-bombers make thirty-eight attacks on Haagsche Bosch.
February 23 to February 26	Only one rocket reaches United Kingdom in more than sixty hours. Rocket-troops and equipment reported leaving Haagsche Bosch for adjacent area Duindigt.
February 24	Air photographs show no rockets Haagsche Bosch; up to six Duindigt.
February 25	Air Ministry warn Chiefs of Staff Germans have new variant of V.1 capable of reaching London from Western Holland.
February 26	Air photographs of Western Holland reveal two ramps aligned London. Third ramp aligned London, and three aligned Antwerp, not seen.
February 27	Hill orders reinforcement of gun-strip east of London.
March 1	Duindigt, with small part of Haagsche Bosch immediately adjacent, heads new V.2 target-list; main part of Haagsche Bosch no longer target.
March 3	Second Tactical Air Force aim sixty-nine tons of bombs at Haagsche Bosch, but miss.
March 3	Ramps in Western Holland open fire on London, inaugurating last phase of V.1 offensive.
March 8	Rocket at Smithfield kills or seriously injures 233 people.

March 20	Hill's fighter-bombers attack ramp at Ypenburg.
March 23	Hill's fighter-bombers repeat attack; fighter-bombers of Second Tactical Air Force attack ramp at Vlaardingen. Both ramps damaged. Third ramp aligned London still not discovered.
March 26 to March 30	Panel of scientists report sympathetically on Pile's project, but Chiefs of Staff reluctant to risk alarming public by large volume of unexplained fire with odds against successs.
March 27: 7.2 a.m.	Rocket at Stepney kills or seriously injures 183 people.
March 27: 4.45 p.m.	Last rocket to reach United Kingdom falls at Orpington, Kent. End of V.2 offensive.
Late March	Rocket-troops leave Holland for Germany.
March 28	Last two flying bombs to reach Greater London fall at Chislehurst and Waltham Cross.
March 29: about 9 a.m.	Last flying bomb to get through defences falls at Datchworth, near Hatfield.
March 29: about 10 a.m.	Last flying bomb to cross coast brought down by anti-aircraft at Iwade, near Sittingbourne.
March 29: 12.43 p.m.	Last flying bomb to approach United Kingdom brought down by anti-aircraft fire off Orfordness. End of V.1 offensive.
April 3	Hill countermands fighter-bomber attacks on V.1 and V.2 targets.
April 13	Radar watch for rockets ceases.
April 25	Hill suspends armed reconnaissance of Western Holland.
May 2	Chiefs of Staff sanction discontinuance of all V.1 and V.2 counter-measures.

May 9   Most of Gruppe Nord and Gruppe Süd surrender to United States Ninth Army. Hill leaves Fighter Command; joins Air Council as Air Member for Technical Services.

Appendix: V.1 and V.2

The FZG. 76, or V.1, was a mid-wing monoplane pilotless aircraft with a wing-span of 16 feet and an overall length of 25 feet. Its all-up weight with the best part of half a ton of fuel aboard was about two tons, the explosive charge in the warhead accounting for rather less than a ton. Its maximum theoretical range was about 160 miles, later increased to nearly 250 miles so that missiles aimed at London could be launched from ramps in Holland. The power-unit, a pulse-jet consisting of an Argus duct modified by incorporation of the valve-system of the Schmidt duct, had a working life of half an hour to an hour. The fuel used was a low-grade aviation spirit.

The missile was not radio-controlled. Launched roughly in the direction of the target, it turned during the first few moments of flight on to a course pre-set on a magnetic compass which monitored an automatic pilot. When a windmill in the nose had made a predetermined number of revolutions a tachometer switched on an electro-mechanical device which swung the missile into a slightly off-course dive.

The usual method of launching was to shoot the missile from a ramp by means of a propulsive device (*Dampferzeuger*) which made use of the powerful reaction between hydrogen peroxide and permanganate of potash, a principle first applied by Professor Hellmut Walter to assisted take-off for aircraft and later extended by him to a variety of other uses. Alternatively the missile could be launched from a specially-modified

Heinkel 111 aircraft. Of roughly 10,500 flying bombs aimed at the United Kingdom in 1944 and 1945, 8,892 were launched from ramps and about 1,600 from aircraft.

The V.1 project appears to have originated with the aero-engine firm of Argus Motorenwerke, and in particular with the design-staff of that firm, headed by Dr Fritz Gosslau. The aircraft firm of Fieseler, who were large users of Argus products, offered to develop the missile and ultimately did so in collab-oration with Argus and with the firm of Askania, who were responsible for the control-mechanism. In March, 1942, Robert Lusser of Fieseler wrote a letter to Dr Gosslau, in which he is understood to have acknowledged that credit for the idea belonged to Argus. Fieseler's offer to the Air Ministry appears to have been made on June 5, 1942; the Air Ministry accepted the project a fortnight later, after an exposition by Dr. Gosslau of its merits. Staff-Engineer Brée was technical co-ordinator on behalf of the Air Ministry, but he is not known to have con-tributed to the design although he may have been responsible for replacement of the valve-mechanism of the Argus duct by that of the Schmidt duct.

About the time when V.1 came into service, rumours were current to the effect that the new weapon was the work of a Belgian inventor. The reference was clearly to Georges Mar-connet, whose pulse-jet was patented in 1910. Dr Gosslau stated after the war that he did not know of Marconnet's work when he and his staff designed the Argus duct, although he became acquainted with it later. Dr Schmidt is said to have studied the book by René Lorin in which jet-propelled missiles were first proposed in detail, but his duct was very different from anything contemplated by Lorin.

The A-4, or V.2, was a gyroscopically-stabilised finned rocket 46 feet long. Its dead weight without fuel, but with a one-ton war-head containing 1,650 lbs. of explosive, was just under four tons. The diameter of the body amidships was nearly five-and-a-half feet; measured over the fins the overall diameter was close on twelve feet. The missile carried roughly four tons of a three-to-one mixture of ethyl alcohol and water and about five tons of liquid oxygen, giving an all-up weight at take-off of nearly thirteen tons. At least two tons of liquid oxygen were lost by evaporation at each launching, so that seven tons or so were needed for every shot. The fuel and oxidant were forced into the combustion-chamber by powerful pumps working on the Hellmut Walter principle and using relatively small quantities of hydrogen peroxide and permanganate.

The maximum range of the A-4 in its standard form was two hundred to two hundred and twenty miles; experimental versions attained ranges of the order of three hundred miles. Aimed at a distant target, the missile reached a height of fifty to sixty miles at the peak of its trajectory, but very much greater heights were attainable where distance was no object. The velocity of the exhaust gases was 6,700 feet a second; that of the missile itself reached a maximum of 3,600 miles an hour and fell to 2,200 to 2,500 miles an hour immediately before impact. The temperature inside the combustion chamber was 2,700 degrees Centigrade.

The missile was launched in an upright position from a portable stand resting on a concrete or other hard surface, and was fuelled and received its final servicing in that posture. It took off under its own power, and appeared to rise very slowly until it gathered momentum from the its 25-ton initial thrust. The figures show, however, that acceleration once the rocket was under way was extremely rapid, rising from 0.9 g immediately after take-off to roughly 5 g at the all-burnt stage. The speed of sound was reached in less than half a minute. Burning-time was of the order of one minute, with a maximum of 65 to 70 seconds for the standard rocket.

The basis of control, as of stability, was the gyroscopic system, which was linked to a set of vanes at the rear of the fins and also to another set placed in the exhaust-stream. The usual method of controlling direction was to pre-set the system so that it held the missile on to the calculated line of shoot by trimming the vanes to correct deviations. Alternatively, the missile could be made to ride a radio-beam in the early stages of its flight, but only where the lie of the land was such that the beam-transmitter could be sited in exactly the right relation to the launching-point.

There were also alternative methods of controlling range. The more elegant method used an integrating accelometer carried in the rocket. This was pre-set to turn off the fuel when the missile, still accelerating, reached a given speed. The gyroscopic system was also pre-set so that its axis shifted from the vertical at a calculated rate as the rocket rose. The rocket was thus made to tilt progressively in such a manner as to put it in precisely the right attitude and position at the crucial moment when it ceased to be an internal combustion machine and became a freely-moving projectile fore-ordained to describe a parabolic curve. If everything was right at that stage, the missile was bound to hit the target unless it blew up first or unless some meteorological factor assumed in the calculations to be negligible proved, after all, significant.

The other method was to cut off the fuel at the appropriate moment by transmitting a radio-impulse from the ground. Whether this gave better timing was a point which the experts seem to have found hard to decide.

Substantially, the A-4 project was planned by Walter Dornberger in 1936 after about five years of study and experiment. From 1932 Dornberger had valuable help from Dr Wernher von Braun, who became his right-hand man and chief collaborator. In his early experiments with rockets propelled by black powder he took as his point of departure the work of such stalwarts of old-time rocketry as the Swedish artillery officer Unge and the Englishman William Hale, who produced about the middle of the nineteenth century a rotating rocket still in use within living memory. Where the 'liquid' rockets on which Dornberger decided in 1932 to found his hopes were concerned, he and von Braun owed more to the theories of the Transylvanian Herman Oberth, himself inspired by the American pioneer Robert Goddard, and to experiments made on a shoestring by a small number of enthusiasts in Germany. These included Oberth, von Braun himself, an engineer named Rudolf Nebel, and the famous Dr Heylandt, who succeeded in propelling a motor-car round Tempelhof aerodrome by means of a jet-propulsion unit which used petrol and liquid oxygen.

In 1938 Dornberger brought in the firm of Siemens to help with the control-mechanism, and after 1939 he was able to draw increasingly on help from academic and commercial sources. For practical purposes, however, he and Wernher von Braun were the parents, inventors, and designers of the rocket. It was they who put mankind on the path to the Sputnik and the planets.

Bibliography and Sources

Books
Babington Smith, Constance, *Evidence in Camera* (1957).
O'Brien, Terence H., *Civil Defence* (1955).
Collier, Basil, *The Defence of the United Kingdom* (1957).
Dornberger, Lieutenant-General Walter, *V-2* (Eng. edn., 1954).
Gatland, Kenneth W., and Kunesch, Anthony M., *Space Travel* (1953).
Gavin, Lieutenant-General James M., *War and Peace in the Space Age* (1959).
Harris, Marshal of the Royal Air Force Sir Arthur, *Bomber Offensive* (1947).
Joubert de la Ferté, Air Chief Marshal Sir Philip, *Rocket* (1957).
Jungk, Robert, *Brighter than a Thousand Suns* (Eng. edn., 1958).
Lorin, René, *L'Air et la Vitesse* (Paris, 1919).
Lusar, Rudolf, *German Secret Weapons of the Second World War* (Eng. edn., 1959).
Oberth, Herman, *Wege Zur Raumschiffahrt* (Munich, 1929).
Saundby, Air Marshal Sir Robert, *Air Bombardment* (1961).
Tully, Andrew, *CIA: The Inside Story* (New York, 1962).

Other Published Material
Goddard, Robert H., *A Method of Reaching Extreme Altitudes* (Washington, 1919); *Liquid Propellant Rocket Development* (Washington, 1936).
Hill, Air Chief Marshal Sir Roderic, *Air Operations by Air Defence of Great Britain and Fighter Command in connection with the German Flying Bomb and Rocket Offensives, 1944–1945* (Supplement to London Gazette, October 19, 1948).

Jones, Professor R. V., *Scientific Intelligence* (Journal of the Royal United Service Institution, August, 1947).

Karavodine, Victor de, *Specification relating to French Patent No. 374,124* (1906).

Marconnet, Georges, *Specification relating to French Patent No. 412,478* (1910).

Index

INDEX